The Limits of Government

The Limits of Government

An Essay on the Public Goods Argument

David Schmidtz

Westview Press
BOULDER • SAN FRANCISCO • OXFORD

Published in 1991 in the United States of America by Westview Press, Inc., 5500 Central Avenue, Boulder, Colorado 80301, and in the United Kingdom by Westview Press, 36 Lonsdale Road, Summertown, Oxford OX2 7EW

Library of Congress Cataloging-in-Publication Data
Schmidtz, David.
The limits of government : an essay on the public goods argument / David Schmidtz.
p. cm.
Includes bibliographical references and index.
ISBN 0-8133-0870-4.—ISBN 0-8133-0871-2 (pbk.)
1. Public goods. I. Title.
HB846.5.S36 1991
338.9—dc20 90-47486
CIP

Printed and bound in the United States of America

The paper used in this publication meets the requirements of the American National Standard for Permanence of Paper for Printed Library Materials Z39.48-1984.

10 9 8 7 6 5 4 3 2 1

To Walter Grinder

Contents

Tables and Figures

Tables

Figures

Preface

In what follows, I discuss what public goods are, why exercising the power of government might be a precondition of public goods production at adequate levels, and when so exercising the power of government might be worth the cost. The most important arguments in the book, in my view, are as follows. Chapter 1 asks what it means to justify the state and finds that there are two incommensurable answers. Chapter 2 then justifies (in one sense) the institution of property. Chapter 3 explains how states can acquire the right to punish those who violate property rights. Presuming the framework of enforceable rights developed in Chapters 2 and 3, Chapter 4 explores a noncoercive solution to the Prisoner's Dilemma and thus to any public goods problems that can be modeled as Prisoner's Dilemmas. Chapter 5 extends the argument of Chapter 4, exploring the moral and strategic complexities of public goods problems that are not Prisoner's Dilemmas.

Chapter 6 concerns, and offers itself as proof of, the possibility of applying the experimental method to moral philosophy. It surveys results of laboratory experiments conducted by several researchers, including me, on the willingness of human subjects to contribute voluntarily to public goods projects. Chapter 7 develops a theory of morality and applies it to questions about public goods. Specifically, when (if ever) are you morally obligated to help produce public goods? When (if ever) are others permitted to force you to help? I conclude that the same considerations that theoretically ground property rights also ground their theoretical limits.

Except where otherwise noted, this book equates individually "rational" action with action that is, strictly speaking, in the agent's self-interest. Let me stress that my intent is merely to conform to standard usage rather than to plump for any substantive theory about what rationality is. In particular, it does not follow from my using the term 'rational' in this way that those who act against self-interest are irrational, but only that if they are rational, then they are rational in some other sense of the term.

I should also stress that the public goods argument is not the sole possible justification of the state. Hence, even if the public goods argument can justify only a minimal state, this does not entail that only a minimal state can be justified. Instead of arguing that the state is justified as a vehicle for promoting public goods production, one might argue that it is justified as a vehicle for promoting, say, equality. Such arguments are not pursued in this book, although I try in passing to note places where alternative arguments might profitably be posed.

Finally, the discussion does not presume any particularly sophisticated conception of the state. I use 'the state' to refer, roughly, to the final civil authority (or claimant thereof) in a given geographical domain. Perhaps, to qualify a claimant as a state, its claim to final civil authority would also need to have been more or less unrivaled in its domain for a number of years. I leave such questions open, for we have nothing to gain by seeking necessary and sufficient conditions for statehood. Indeed, I doubt that what we mean when we use the term is precise enough to admit of such conditions. But for a discussion of the functional and historical properties that might suffice to *justify* a state, please turn to Chapter 1.

Acknowledgments

I gratefully acknowledge financial support from several sources. Chapters 4 and 6 grew out of my dissertation. A Leonard P. Cassidy Fellowship in Law and Philosophy from the Institute for Humane Studies helped me write the former. The latter discusses experimental research by Mark Isaac, David Schmidtz and James Walker, which was financed by the National Science Foundation (SES 8606770 and 86081121) and the Alfred P. Sloan Foundation. I have a special debt to my collaborator, mentor, and friend, Mark Isaac, for securing these grants and for introducing me to experimental economics. I wrote most of Chapters 3 and 7 during the summer of 1989 while in residence at the Social Philosophy and Policy Center at Bowling Green State University. It was a summer of uninterrupted working days followed by warm summer evenings of wine and conversation with friends from the Philosophy Department. I have seldom been so thoroughly content. A John F. Enders Grant from Yale University covered expenses during the project's final stages.

I thank the following journals for permission to use previously published material. A forerunner of Chapter 4 appeared in the *Harvard Journal of Law and Public Policy* (1987a). A paper appearing in *Philosophical Papers* (1988) inspires the first section of Chapter 5. Chapter 3's section on peace as a public good uses material from *Philosophia* (1989). The sections in Chapter 1 on justification and hypothetical consent draw on material from *Ethics* (1990, copyright by The University of Chicago. 0014-1701/91/0101-0001).

I thank Allen Buchanan, under whose direction I finished my dissertation, and Holly Smith, without whom I would not have been given the chance to begin. I thank Spencer Carr for overcoming my reluctance to show him my dissertation, for convincing me that it was worth revising, and for working so hard to make this a better book. What a luxury to have a philosopher of his caliber as an editor.

Tyler Cowen, Gregory Kavka, Christopher Morris, Alan Nelson, and Elizabeth Willott commented on the entire manuscript. I received comments on one or more chapters from Lawrence Becker, Mike Bradie, Phil Bricker, Grant Brown, Allen Buchanan, Keith Burgess-Jackson, Jim Child, Jules Coleman, Kenneth Cust, Scott Davidson, Bob Dorsey, Ivan Fox, Ken Gemes, Joel Feinberg, Raymond Frey, Mark Isaac, Russell Landau, Keith Lehrer, Roderick Long, Mark Migotti, Fred Miller, Gerald Postema, Carol Rovane, Jeremy Shearmur, John Simmons, Holly Smith, Scott Sturgeon, Jim Taylor, and Rod Wiltshire. I thank them all.

A number of students at Yale also took a lively and critical interest in the manuscript and had a significant influence on the final product. Among those whom I should single out for special thanks are Laura Ballard, Jon Gordon, Jessica Greenfield, Von Hughes, Theo Liebman, David Massey, Gabriel Mesa, Nathaniel Sears, Ray Shepherd, and David Steinberg. My thanks also to Beverly LeSuer, Margo Reeves, Sheldon L. Richman, and Ida May Norton for helping me prepare the final copy of this manuscript.

Most of all, I wish to thank Dr. Elizabeth Willott for caring about what I do and for gracing my life with her delightfully unpredictable ways.

The Limits of Government

1

The Public Goods Argument

Society runs itself. As long as a system of property rights protects and gives meaning to people's right to be left in peace, individual initiative will produce the essential elements of human flourishing. The trouble is, this liberal insight presupposes the efficacy of markets, and markets can fail. In particular, the fabric of social harmony, woven by markets from threads of self-interested action, may prove too delicate when it comes to producing public goods.

Therein lies a role for government. According to Mancur Olson, "A state is first of all an organization that provides public goods for its members, the citizens" (1965, p. 15). A public good, roughly speaking, is a good that can be produced only by collective action, but its production benefits people regardless of whether they join in the collective effort. Such collective action as is necessary to provide public goods is collectively rational in a straightforward sense. Even so, it is often not *individually* rational for people voluntarily to do their part to secure a collectively rational outcome. (After all, why not enjoy the benefits of other people's efforts for free?) Assuming people typically do what is individually rational, the moral justification for coercive provision of public goods is also relatively straightforward. We need only argue (or so it might seem) for a particularly benign kind of paternalism.

To wit, we all want public goods, but we know perfectly well that many of us will not voluntarily contribute to their production.

Thus, compelling us to contribute is paternalistic insofar as it does something for each of us that is good for us but that we cannot do for ourselves because we lack the collective will. (More precisely, each of us could will ourselves to act individually, but what we really want is to act collectively, and sometimes there is no will among us that can move us to act collectively.) Narrowly described acts of taking *your* money are not done for your good, but more broadly described acts of taking your money and everyone else's too are done for your good and for everyone else's too. This paternalism is benign in the sense that the end it helps us attain is not only good for us but is also an end we actually desire. We all *want* the government to force each of us to contribute and thereby make us better off. Even if no one desires that the government take his or her own money, it might nevertheless be true that everyone desires that the government takes everyone's money. Michael Taylor sums it up: "The most persuasive justification of the state is founded on the argument that, without it, people would not successfully cooperate in realizing their common interests and in particular would not provide themselves with certain public goods" (1987, p. 1). This, in essence, is the public goods argument.

The public goods argument has more familiarity and wider acceptance among economists and political scientists than it has among philosophers, at least in its modern and rather technical incarnation.[1] Nevertheless, the argument has had a major influence on political philosophy since the time it was implicitly put forth by Thomas Hobbes.[2] Hobbes argued that *peace* is, in effect, a universally desired public good, because securing it is a prerequisite of self-preservation; even so, individual rationality counsels people to seek the advantages of war, unless they are able to establish by covenant an overarching power to keep the peace by holding the multitude in awe. (See Hobbes, chaps. 13 and 17.)

Two Kinds of Justification

We return in Chapter 2 and especially Chapter 3 to the problem of how to produce the public good of peace. Here, we must pause to consider a more general issue. What does the public goods argument have to do with justifying the state? What sort of work is the public goods argument supposed to do? It turns out that there is more than one possibility. Hobbes is usually classified as a contractarian—someone who argues that a state is justified either by obtaining the consent of its citizens or by being the kind of state to which rational people would consent under the right conditions. (These two versions of contractarianism may be labeled *actual consent* and *hypothetical consent* arguments, respectively.) Because the public goods argument has its philosophical roots in Hobbes, it would be natural to assume that the public goods argument is a contractarian argument.

We should, however, resist this temptation. To see why, we must distinguish what I see as two different methods of justification in political theory. I call the two methods *teleological* and *emergent* justification. The teleological approach seeks to justify institutions in terms of what they accomplish. The emergent approach regards justification as a property that emerges from the process by which institutions arise.[3]

Teleological justification posits *goals* and compares the practicably attainable forms of government in terms of how they do or will serve those goals. In contrast, emergent justification posits *constraints* of a particular kind—namely constraints on the process by which the state comes to be. Emergent justification turns on a state's pedigree. It is not essentially comparative, although comparing states in terms of their relative success in meeting a standard of emergent justification is by no means ruled out.

Consider some examples. Following Hobbes, one might argue that instituting a Leviathan is teleologically justified if a war of all against all would otherwise be inevitable. In contrast, a Hobbesian might argue that a Leviathan will be emergently justified if it emerges from the state of nature by consent. (For the moment, think of the appeal as being to actual or tacit consent. I discuss hypothetical consent arguments in the next section.) This emergent approach has both invisible-hand and contractarian versions. In the former, the Leviathan's emergence is an unintended result of people individually binding themselves to a prince. In the latter, people bind themselves by collective agreement. To show that a state actually emerged by consent would be a very strong form of emergent justification. At the same time, showing that it did not satisfy this stringent standard would be correspondingly weak as a basis for condemnation. In contrast, to show that a state emerged without violating rights would be a relatively weak emergent justification, but by the same token, showing that a state's emergence did not satisfy even this minimal standard would be the basis for a relatively strong condemnation.

Particular institutions within the state can also be justified by either teleological or emergent methods. For example, one could try to teleologically justify creating a standing army by arguing that the army will provide the paradigmatic public good of national defense. Or one could try to emergently justify creating a standing army by showing that its creation was duly approved by the appropriate legislative bodies. To have emergent justificatory significance, the legislative process must not violate moral borders. (I use the phrase 'moral borders' to refer to rights in particular and also to anything else that separates what can permissibly be done to a person from what cannot.) This leaves open the question of whether the process's significance derives from the property of not violating moral borders or from some other property, but in either case, if the process violates moral borders, this will undermine such emergent justificatory significance as it would otherwise have had.

Neither teleological nor emergent models are normatively self-contained. The teleological approach presupposes the legitimacy of certain goals. The emergent approach presupposes certain constraints applying to processes by which states arise. One might suppose that the teleological approach essentially ignores moral borders, but this is not so. Both approaches presume some sort of position on the nature of moral borders around persons—in the one case because the state can be judged according to whether its emergence leaves such borders intact, in the other case because the state can be judged according to how well it serves the goal of protecting them. (Among the positions that a utilitarian version of the teleological approach may take, of course, is the position that rights in particular and perhaps even moral borders in general are "nonsense on stilts.")

Needless to say, chains of justification must come to an end, and no chain has enough links in it to satisfy everyone. But we can, in principle at least, specify how the two approaches to justifying the state link up to ethics in general (See Chapter 7 as well.) Although neither approach is normatively self-contained, it would be a mistake to infer that the teleological approach presupposes a consequentialist moral theory and the emergent approach a deontological one. Consequentialists naturally endorse the teleological approach to justifying the state, but a consequentialist might insist that both kinds of justification are essential, out of a belief that if we do not insist that institutions be emergently justified, the institutions we ultimately end up with will not be teleologically justified either. An institution whose emergence tramples moral borders will probably trample moral borders as long as it exists—or so a consequentialist who cares about moral borders might reasonably fear. So the emergent approach can appeal to consequentialists and deontologists alike.

The teleological approach can be of similarly broad appeal. Note that an emergent justification couched in terms of moral borders would begin and end with an argument that the process of emergence itself did not violate moral borders. Some deontologists may conclude that a strong enough emergent justification is sufficient in itself to underwrite the institution's claim to support. On the other hand, everyone cares about how governments perform, including Kantians. When deontologists ask if the maxim "Support institution X" can be universalized, they are not asking about the consequences of their contemplated support. Yet, the maxim's meaning will still depend on the nature of institution X. And it would not be inconsistent with deontology to notice that institutions can and sometimes must be defined partly in terms of their functional properties. A deontologist may hold that the state's function—indeed its duty—is to protect moral borders around persons and then to leave citizens to do as they please within those borders. Where a consequentialist would hold that the state's purpose is to promote the good, a deontologist may hold that the state's purpose is to promote the right. Deontologists typically would not hold that the purpose of *persons* is to promote the right, for persons are ends in themselves. But states are not ends in themselves, or at least a deontologist need not view them as such. Deontologists may consistently judge that a state that protects moral borders satisfies such conditions as are necessary for it to command their support. At the same time, most deontologists would not consider possession of this functional property alone sufficient, for they would denounce a group that initially ran roughshod over moral borders so as to create and solidify the political power base that subsequently enabled the group (now calling itself a government) to effectively protect moral borders. Thus, like some of their consequentialist colleagues, deontologists may judge that, to command their support, an institution must be both teleologically and emergently justified.

The fact that there are two kinds of justification, however, implies that there may be institutions that are justified in one sense but not in the other. Thus, even a state that has emerged by actual consent is subject to criticism on the basis of how it functions; even a state that functions exceedingly well can be criticized on the basis of what it did to acquire such efficacy. Is there such a thing as a neutral court in which teleological and emergent approaches can square off against each other, yielding a final score that will tell us whether an institution is justified in an overall sense? As far as I can tell, the answer is no. There is no neutral court, no third "overall" sense of justification. Rather, in cases of conflict, one approach can carry the day against the other only on its own terms. That a successful justification is merely a justification on its own terms means that even a successful justification is not a conversation stopper.

Of course, it will not surprise anyone to learn that conversation stoppers are hard to come by in political debate, but this analysis at least suggests what is often going on when a debate appears to have no resolution. Consider the debate over the legitimacy of affirmative action programs. Among the many arguments that can be mustered on either side is the following: Legislation that discriminates against people on the basis of race or gender is wrong; it crosses moral borders (for such borders are to be found around everyone, not only members of currently favored minorities).

Hence, because legislators do not have the right to pass such laws, legislation merely cloaks affirmative action statutes in the garb of emergent justification. Such statutes cannot be emergently justified. A converse argument follows these lines: Unequal opportunity at present will have better results (in terms of preference satisfaction, equality of result, or equality of opportunity in the long run) than would equal opportunity, assuming that such remedial legislation more quickly negates the results of unequal opportunity in the past. Hence, affirmative action is teleologically justified. Note that these two conclusions pass each other like ships in the night. They might both be false.

But suppose they are both true. I am not saying that there is some question of overall justification the answer to which remains unresolved. There is no such question. When the two approaches yield different conclusions about the justification of a particular institution, no overarching third sense of justification exists to settle the issue. One can only say that if an institution is not emergently justified, it had better be teleologically justified, and vice versa. One stops the conversation if—and not until—one justifies an institution in both senses of the term.

On the other hand, when the issue concerns the nature of justification itself rather than the justification of particular institutions, abandoning the idea of an overarching sense of justice is often what makes settling the issue possible. For example, suppose we consider the ages-old question "Can the end justify the means?" If we do not distinguish between teleological and emergent justification, we will be conflating two quite different questions. There will be no answer. Once we distinguish between teleological and emergent justification, however, the two questions become well-defined and tractable. If we mean "Can the end teleologically justify the means?" then the answer is yes. If we mean "Can the end emergently justify the means?" then the answer is no.[4]

Hypothetical Consent

Having distinguished between teleological and emergent justification, we now return to the question of whether the public goods argument can usefully be understood as a hypothetical consent argument. As an example of an argument that might be so understood, consider the following:

(1) If the state, and only the state, can adequately provide public goods, then rational bargainers would consent to the state.
(2) The state, and only the state, can adequately provide public goods. Therefore,
(3) Rational bargainers would consent to the state.

Once we recognize that emergent and teleological approaches are two separate methods of justification, two things happen. First, we see that hypothetical consent arguments have no bearing on emergent justification, for a state can only be emergently justified in terms of the process by which it actually arose. David Hume (1965) was right to reject hypothetical consent arguments as irrelevant fiction, at least if we see hypothetical consent arguments as attempts at emergent justification.

Second, if we instead understand the hypothetical consent story as an attempted teleological justification, we see that Hume's objection is no objection at all. The point of the story would be to compare the state to its alternatives rather than to give an account of its history. Hypothetical consent arguments are no less problematic as attempts at teleological justification, but for a different reason: If we view the hypothetical consent argument as an attempted teleological justification, we see that the real work being done in the argument from (1) to (3) is the teleological work of premise (2). Once we have (2), nothing is added by going on to get (3).

Of course, consent can be a *sign* that being subject to the state is preferable to going without public goods. More generally, consent can be a sign that a government is teleologically justified. (I.e., what warrants hypothesizing consent in the first place is that people would have good reasons to consent.) But a government can be teleologically justified even if collective action problems would prevent the sign of its justification from materializing. Admittedly, the likelihood of strategically minded individuals holding out for special concessions from the rest of the group threatens to falsify (1), for it suggests that even bargainers who see an urgent need to create a state might still have rational reasons to impede its creation by holding out for special favors. If hypothetical consent could offer the possibility of emergent justification, there would be a point in trying to find ways around this problem. Such concerns, however, are utterly irrelevant to the state's teleological justification, for the falsehood of (1) presents an obstacle only to moving from (2) to (3). But, once we have (2), nothing is gained by moving to (3). Therefore, it makes no difference to the state's teleological justification whether (1) is true or false.

Thus, the hypothetical consent argument is as irrelevant to teleological justification as it is to emergent justification. Premise (2)'s truth-value is relevant to the state's teleological justification, but the argument as a whole is not. Either we already have a teleological justification in (2), in which case we do not need the hypothetical consent in (3), or if we seek consent as a sign of teleological justification, we cannot produce the sign until we first produce a teleological justification as a basis for hypothesizing the sign.

More generally, if we actually observe people consenting, then that in itself is reason to expect that they would consent under similar circumstances. Absent such observations, we must never simply assume that people would consent to something; we have to give reasons why they would or should consent. (So if I say the state is justified with respect to you because you would have consented to it under the appropriate conditions, you might quite reasonably respond by asking, "What makes you think I would have consented?" My answer would have to be that a rational person such as yourself would have good reasons to consent.) If we discover a good reason why people should consent to the state—call it "reason X"—we will then be free to contrive hypothetical stories about rational agents reacting to reason X by consenting to the state, but the real story will already have been told by reason X itself. (The hypothetical story adds nothing whatsoever. It certainly does not add consent, for the story is only hypothetical.) In other words, hypothetical consent cannot constitute justification; to suppose hypothetical consent is to presuppose justification. Hypothetical consent proceeds *from* teleological justification rather than *to* it.

Thus, it is worth stressing that there are straightforwardly teleological approaches to justifying the state. The public goods argument is one of them. Securing consent to the state is not the argument's purpose. The argument does not need to be embedded in the contractarian enterprise. David Hume's version of the public goods argument, to give one example, divorces itself from the contractarian trappings of its antecedents.

Hume seems to say that the beauty of the state is not that it results from a collective decision but rather that it makes collective decisions unnecessary. People no longer need to come to an agreement about what is in their collective interest, for magistrates "need consult no body but themselves to form any scheme for the promoting of that interest.... Thus, bridges are built; harbours open'd; ramparts rais'd; canals form'd; fleets equip'd; and armies disciplin'd; every where, by the care of government, which, tho' compos'd of men subject to all human infirmities, becomes, by one of the finest and most subtle inventions imaginable, a composition, that is, in some measure, exempted from all these infirmities" (Hume, 1978, p. 539). Hume's point is not that people consent to government, but rather that government does something that needs doing. Moreover, Hume's version of the argument is the most fundamental because if it does not establish that government does something that needs doing, the associated contractarian argument—that people have reason to consent to government—does not get off the ground.

Voluntary Methods of Public Goods Provision

From Hume's point of view, then, the attractiveness of government fundraising methods is that they eliminate the difficult step of getting people to agree to contribute. Instead, funds are typically raised through various kinds of taxation. Because we will be construing the public goods argument as a teleological approach to justifying the state's employment of such methods, it will be necessary to compare these methods to the alternatives. Thus, one way in which this book engages the public goods argument is by exploring voluntary methods of public goods provision.

The fundamental thrust of the public goods argument is that the state does something that needs doing. Studying voluntary mechanisms is a means of making sure that what needs doing really needs to be done *by the state*. An even more important reason to study voluntary mechanisms, perhaps, is that not everything *can* be done by the state. No matter how much people prefer to rely on government to provide them with public goods, a substantial reliance on voluntary cooperation is inevitable, and a well-functioning society needs to know how to make voluntary mechanisms as efficient as possible.

For example, consider the so-called greenhouse effect. As I write, some (although by no means all) experts believe that the burning of fossil fuels is significantly increasing atmospheric concentrations of carbon dioxide. The carbon dioxide absorbs energy from ultraviolet radiation reflected by the planet's surface that would otherwise escape into space. As a result, the earth's temperature is rising. Moreover, people are destroying the forests and ocean algae that metabolize carbon dioxide and maintain atmospheric oxygen levels, which is something that previous models had not taken into account. (Previous models took increased carbon dioxide production into account but not decreasing oxygen production.) Some researchers worry that the changing climate will itself eventually begin to decimate forests (Roberts, 1988). If they are right, we will soon be living in a world that will strike even the most casual observer as suboptimal.

If the greenhouse effect is real, then halting and reversing it would be a public good. But the problem would be international. Outright coercion at this level is not an option. The depletion of the upper atmosphere's ozone layer presents the same kind of problem. Perhaps the U.S. government is in a position to coerce U.S. industries into curtailing the use of fluorocarbons (currently thought to be causing the ozone problem in part), but is it in any position to coerce Japanese and Soviet industries? Here too, if the problem turns out to be as bad as some scientists fear, an international policy will be needed, and implementing it by force is hardly possible. In this case, dismissing voluntary methods of public goods provision as impractical is not an option, because there are cases, far too important to ignore, where voluntary methods are all we have.

Halting the proliferation of nuclear arms would also be a public good. A given country could help to produce this good by curtailing its own production of nuclear arms, but by doing so, it would be helping to make the world safer for those who are part of the problem (and giving them a strategic military advantage to boot) as well as for those who are part of the solution. In the case of the public good of nuclear disarmament, the willingness to use force is the problem rather than the solution.

On a more local scale, coercion becomes a practical possibility, but it is by no means always appropriate to the circumstances. The threat of flooding in recent years in Salt Lake City, Utah, has more than once led hundreds of volunteers to put in long hours erecting sandbag dikes to protect the city and keep its highways open. The government could have preempted this by raising taxes, using the proceeds to finance a standing army of flood fighters. But would those people who helped save the city with their own two hands feel the same way if they had instead participated by being sources of government revenue? Not at all. Here a certain value and a certain efficiency cry out for study: Why does voluntary provision of public goods occur? How effective is it, both absolutely and in comparison to coercive alternatives? How might it be nurtured?

Justification and Consent

Distinguishing between teleological and emergent justification has helped us see that hypothetical consent arguments are combinations of two separable strands of argument. The emergent strand has no justificatory potential, however, because a government can be emergently justified only by reference to the process by which it actually arose. Emergent justifications are immensely important in both political theory and political practice, but the gesture that hypothetical consent arguments make in the direction of providing an emergent justification is spurious. An institution's emergent justification will be found in the institution's actual history or it will not be found at all. The teleological strand of the hypothetical consent argument has justificatory potential, but the realization of this potential is presupposed by rather than supplied by the argument that rational agents would consent under the hypothesized circumstances.

Although the subject of this book, the public goods argument, is fundamentally an attempt to justify the state teleologically, by no means is the possibility of emergent justification being abandoned. Nor do I mean to slight the significance of emergent justification. On the contrary, unlike hypothetical consent, actual consent has justificatory force above and beyond the teleological force of the reasons people have for consenting. Freely given consent is intrinsically a kind of authorization; by consenting, we give others a right to expect from us that which we have consented to do or to give.

There is also another sense in which the least problematic kind of emergent justification consists of showing that an institution arose by consent. Because a necessary condition of an institution's emergent justification is that it must emerge without violating rights, any attempt at emergent justification can ordinarily be rebutted by showing that the process of emergence violated rights. The process of emerging by consent is very special in this respect, however, for consent is its own proof against rebuttal. If a state arises by unanimous consent, the only rights its emergence can violate are those that cannot be alienated by consent. Hence, most, if not all, of the claims about rights violations that might have rebutted the state's emergent justification will have been dealt with at a stroke.

The trouble, of course, is that we do not observe this sort of consent on a large enough scale to justify the state. Thus, we must consider whether there are nonconsensual processes by which states might emerge without violating rights. Chapters 2 and 3 undertake the emergent justification of the institutionalization of property and punishment, respectively. Both arguments serve as examples of how institutions that supply critically important public goods can be emergently justified, despite the fact that they did not emerge by consent.

2

Property

Original Appropriation

Property typically comes to us by transfer from previous owners. All property, however, eventually traces its existence (as property) to appropriations of previously unowned goods. Ultimately, then, whether the institution of property can be emergently justified depends on whether original appropriation can be justified. This raises a problem. Chapter 1 suggested that an institution is emergently justified if it arises by actual consent. Original appropriation, however, cannot be emergently justified in this fashion; when one acquires property by original appropriation, there are, by definition, no previous owners from whom one could obtain consent. So how can original appropriation be emergently justified? Are there nonconsensual processes by which an institution might emerge in a justified way?

Nonconsensual modes of emergent justification are the subject of this chapter and Chapter 3. In this chapter, I argue that original appropriation can be justified. Because those who find original appropriation problematic usually rest their case on the apparent impossibility of satisfying the so-called Lockean Proviso, it is important to explore its logic. I do so in this chapter.

Notice that although original appropriation must be justified if property is to be emergently justified, this does not dictate that original appropriation must be *emergently* justified. In other words, a principle that specifies how institutions may legitimately arise is a principle of emergent justification. If we then ask why we are using that particular principle rather than some alternative, we may say the principle is one we all agreed to use. Or we may say that using that principle has the best results. But although our *rationales* for the principle may be either emergent or teleological, it remains the case that the principle we are trying to rationalize is, after all, still a principle that specifies how institutions may legitimately arise. Hence, regardless of what we deem to be *its* rationale, it is still a principle of emergent justification.

For example, being ratified by a constitutionally bound legislative body is one way in which an institution can be emergently justified. Yet, although we look to the legislative body as a vehicle for emergent justification, we remain free to judge the legislative body itself in terms of how it functions, as well as in terms of how it emerged. Moreover, some criteria of emergent justification do not emerge by human action at all—hence the non-event of their emergence can neither be defended nor criticized. We could, for example, claim that we have certain rights by nature and that, to be emergently justified, a state must emerge without violating them. We could not emergently justify natural rights claims, however, for their emergence is not an issue. Unless there is a third alternative, we would have to justify them teleologically.

These thoughts suggest an interesting possibility: Emergent justification of property can be based on a principle of original appropriation that is itself teleologically justified. Indeed, I argue here that there are solid teleological reasons why original appropriation is permissible. If I am correct, then the institution of property can be emergently justified as having come into being through a series of permissible original appropriations. This constitutes an emergent justification of property despite the fact that its criterion of emergent justification (i.e., of original appropriation) is in turn justified teleologically. Conventions of property comprise the first example of a public good important enough and obvious enough that its teleological justification reshapes such moral borders as would otherwise render its emergent justification impossible, in particular changing the conditions under which consent is required.[1]

The Lockean Proviso

Under what conditions, then, can removing natural resources from the common stock be justified? The standard answer is John Locke's: "Labour being the unquestionable Property of the Labourer, no Man but he can have a right to what that is once joyned to, at least where there is enough, and as good left in common for others" (1963, p. 329).

Thus, the way to remove resources from the common stock is to mix one's labor with them, thereby annexing them to one's person. A problematic idea, to be sure, but what is interesting is how Locke qualifies it: However one goes about removing goods from the commons, one can establish unequivocal title to those goods only if one's act of removal leaves "enough and as good" for others. This qualification upon what one can originally extract from the commons is now known as the *Lockean Proviso*.

Virtually no one, to my knowledge, believes that any particular act of initial appropriation, in a world of scarcity, stands much chance of satisfying the Lockean Proviso.[2] Judith Jarvis Thomson once put it this way:

> I suspect that there is no plausible construal of what Locke had in mind by 'enough, and as good' under which anyone's taking land for himself would leave enough and as good for all the other owners. (For one thing, Locke did not realize how large the class of owners was going to be.) I therefore suspect that if we take leaving enough and as good as a *necessary* condition for property acquisition, then it will follow that there can be no private ownership of land. (Thomson, 1976, p. 666)

Jeremy Waldron concurs:

> If the 'enough and as good' clause were a necessary condition on appropriation, it would follow that, in these circumstances, the only legitimate course for the inhabitants would be death by starvation and exposure of them all (distribution by consent being ruled out practically and *ex hypothesi*), since *no* ap-

> propriation would leave enough and as good in common for others. (Waldron, 1979, p. 325)

Likewise, Rolf Sartorius says this: "Understood as an original limitation upon the right to appropriate natural resources, the condition that 'there be enough and as good left for others' could not of course be literally satisfied by any system of private property rights" (Sartorius, 1984, p. 210).

We compound the problem, as John T. Sanders explains, if we suppose (quite reasonably) that the Proviso requires us to leave something for our children as well as for each other. In particular, "if you consider *all* future generations, and if you must leave enough and as good for every future human being, then it is hard to imagine that the Proviso would allow you to mix your labor with much more than an infinitesimal slice of land" (Sanders, 1987, p. 377).

The view of Thomson, Waldron, Sartorius, and Sanders comes as close to reflecting a genuine consensus as views in political philosophy ever get. John Arthur adds that "if one approaches the problem of resource acquisition from the perspective of the Lockean 'proviso', that enough and as good must be left in common, then the typical method of acquiring property under capitalism is unjust" (Arthur, 1987, pp. 337-338). If Arthur is right, the implications are far-reaching indeed. If no initial acquisitions at all can be legitimate, private holdings are illegitimate in principle. "A stolen bicycle, even if it were freely given to you by a generous thief, is not yours to keep; the illegitimate step in the process casts a shadow across all subsequent transactions. An illegitimate original acquisition would similarly infect all subsequent transfers" (Arthur, 1987, p. 338).

Sanders takes a similar view of the issue's significance:

> That some initial claim to property be defensible is required by any theory that holds that certain present distributions may be justified, that certain transfers of property are justified, or that restitution ought to be made for previous injustice in transfer or acquisition. The initial acquisition of property, and its justification, is crucial to the remainder of property theory. (Sanders, 1987, p. 369)

The apparent impossibility of satisfying the Proviso, then, has genuinely startling implications. Private property, moreover, is only one of many institutions whose legitimacy is called into question by this line of argument. The appropriation of land by worker communes is subject to the same objection. Likewise, reserving a campsite in a crowded national park also fails to leave enough and as good for others, as does the use of public property in general when such property is subject to rationing or crowding. Restrictions on immigration are problematic for the same reason: By instituting them, we fail to leave enough and as good for those who, as a result, find themselves on the outside looking in.

The institutions mentioned are all ways of establishing control over territory. In particular, they establish the power and assume the right to restrict access to territory to which access was once unrestricted—they remove such territory from the commons. (So a person or group effectively removes or appropriates goods from the commons by establishing control over them, establishing in particular the power to exclude others from consuming those goods.) If the institution of private property falls to the objection that original appropriation cannot be justified, it falls as a method of restricting access to the commons, and all methods of restricting access to the commons fall along with it. Unless we are willing to admit that no such institutions can be legitimate, we seem forced to dismiss the Proviso as, at best, a sufficient but not necessary condition on appropriation that, being impossible to satisfy, should be ignored. Indeed, Sanders (1987, pp. 380ff) has a powerful argument that ignoring it is exactly what we should do.

Against the idea that we should ignore the Proviso, consider that in proposing it, Locke is already retreating from the usual criterion of legitimate property *transfer*, which requires that transactions be consensual. The retreat is necessary because a would-be original appropriator cannot obtain the prior consent of previous owners before assuming control over the resource. By hypothesis, there are no previous owners. Nor does anyone have the kind of claim to the resource that prior owners would have, so there is no reason to suppose that anything as strong as prior consent is normatively required to legitimize original appropriation.

Yet Locke was right to think *something* must be done to justify original appropriation, for such appropriation seizes exclusive control over that to which others previously had unrestricted access. Especially under conditions of scarcity, such seizures must be justified. Locke is also basically on target in specifying the nature of the required justification—one should not appropriate goods from the commons without stopping to consider what one is leaving for others. Robert Nozick agrees, saying that any adequate theory of justice in acquisition will contain something like the Proviso (Nozick, 1974, p. 178). The trouble is that, as J.H. Bogart says, under conditions of scarcity, "every acquisition worsens the lot of others—and worsens their lot in relevant ways" (Bogart, 1985, p. 834). The Proviso appears, contrary to Locke's intention, no less stringent than the requirement that one obtain the prior consent of others. Both appear to be tests that original appropriation cannot possibly pass.

Suppose it really is necessary for original appropriation to satisfy the Proviso. Would justifying original appropriation be possible? I think so. Moreover, I do not think it becomes harder for original appropriation to satisfy the Proviso the scarcer goods become. In fact, far from never *permitting* us to remove goods from the commons, the Proviso may sometimes *require* us to take that very action. I do not claim that Locke himself intended the Proviso to be read as I read it. Nevertheless, I believe the Proviso should be read this way, because this reading captures a crucial truth about the conditions under which property is legitimate.

A Tragedy in Eden

Imagine that a group of us find ourselves instantiated in a valley full of various kinds of apple trees, some of which already bear ripe fruit. Finding ourselves hungry, we commence to picking and eating apples. But some apples are better than others, so as other trees begin to ripen, a few of us rush to pick the best apples. In fact, we pick them before they are quite ripe, and the other people dash in, fearing that they will otherwise lose out entirely. The pace of this race inevitably quickens, and eventually we find ourselves picking fruit before it is really edible. If we do not, someone else will snatch it first, and (by the smallest of margins) we would rather have little green apples than none at all.

Tired of this degrading affair and of being underfed, one of us—Jane is her name—builds a fence around a single blossoming tree. The rest of us pay little attention to Jane until the day approaches when her tree—the only tree we have yet to ravage—will bear the only ripe apples in the valley. There are those of us who think about killing her in her sleep. But there are others who decide that her idea was a good one and follow suit while there is still time. Some of us claim plots of land as individuals. Some of us, in groups, claim plots jointly, adopting various ways of sharing the costs and benefits of joint management. (The details of our arrangements are not important here. The task at hand is to justify original appropriation in general rather than to justify any particular kind of property institution.)

Then Group II comes along. They find some trees fenced off and bearing lots of ripe fruit. The rest of the trees have been destroyed. (We tore them down trying to eat the bark.) Group II approaches the fenced-off trees and asks us where Group II's trees are. We say there are no trees for Group II. Group II says, "But we are hungry." We say, "No problem. Grab those old dead trees over there and make fence posts. We'll trade apples for them." Group II says, "All right, but there are many groups yet to come. There aren't enough apples to feed them all." Hearing this, and remembering all too well what famine is like, we begin to tremble a bit. Well, except for Jane. She is thinking about the new fence post industry and how it will facilitate the reclamation and rehabilitation of land for agricultural use. The end of our story finds her busy collecting apple seeds.

The moral of the story is this: As latecomers arrive and natural resources become scarce, anything left in the commons will be leveled. This much is not news, at least not to readers of Garrett Hardin.[3] What really is news is this: *Leaving goods in the commons fails to satisfy the Proviso*. In fact, leaving goods in the commons practically ensures their ruin. The essence of what Hardin calls the

Tragedy of the Commons—what makes it tragic—is *precisely* that not enough and as good is left for others. As a necessary condition for satisfying the Proviso, goods *must* be removed from the commons. Moreover, the more severe the scarcity, the faster resources will be destroyed in the commons, and thus the more urgently the Proviso will *require* that resources be removed from the commons.

Needless to say, there is more than one institutional framework that can effectively remove goods from the commons, ranging from private property to public property to national borders. For present purposes, this makes no difference. We are not trying to decide which institutions are most effective or even which are justified; our mission is only to show that the establishment of exclusive control, which they all presume, can be justified.

At any rate, there is no incentive to nurture apple trees in the commons; in the commons, the fruits of production belong to others as much as to oneself. If one does not want to starve, one is better off spending one's time eating (while one can) rather than producing. If only we had the power to decide how everyone will act, there might not be any point in removing resources from the commons. We could satisfy the Proviso by choosing for everyone to abide by principles of efficient and equitable harvesting. But we choose for ourselves, not for everyone. And what people should choose for themselves differs from what would be just (and from what the Proviso would require) if they were choosing for everyone.

What does this general point imply about the commons? The commons might never be leveled if we could choose for everyone to leave enough and as good for others. But people choose for themselves, which makes a difference to what can count as leaving enough and as good for others. (To decide that everyone will leave a piece of land alone would be to protect it; to decide to leave it alone oneself is merely to leave it unprotected.) In the commons, we could naively restrain ourselves, waiting our turn and then eating only our share. But that would be pointless. Those who do otherwise will still precipitate the commons tragedy. Our only choices in this unfolding tragedy would be these: (1) join in the mad rush to mutual starvation, (2) refuse to join the rush and be the first to starve, or (3) stake a claim we can defend, rhetorically and otherwise. Only if some people successfully implement the third choice is there any chance the Proviso can be satisfied.

Are those who initially catalyze this mad rush doing something wrong? Probably, but whether their actions are right or wrong is not really the point. The point is that until access to the land is restricted, people will have the opportunity and the incentive to overuse it, and some of them as a matter of fact will overuse it, thereby not leaving enough and as good for others. When some people overuse the commons, the stock of what is left for others will decrease, progressively tending to push others to the point where even modest consumption levels on their part cumulatively exceed sustainable yields, so that everyone who appropriates apples from the commons eventually comes to contribute to the tragedy—and possibly starves to boot. (All of this is greatly exacerbated, of course, by the lack of incentive to make use of the common land's latent productive capacity. In the commons, one acquires things not by producing them but rather by grabbing them. And right or wrong, simply grabbing is not, in and of itself, very productive.)

If one is to satisfy the Proviso in a way that has some positive bearing on the preservation of the human race, one must, first and foremost, satisfy the Proviso insofar as it applies to things like apples, i.e., food. But if one merely appropriates apples, one is not satisfying the Proviso with respect to apples. Those who appropriate apples from the commons violate the Proviso (under any interpretation of it) insofar as it pertains to apples, and so generate the commons tragedy.

The next step is to realize that the looming tragedy with respect to apples alters what the Proviso means as a constraint on appropriations of land. In other words, some alteration of the rules of access to apples is necessary if the Proviso with respect to apples is to be satisfied. The Proviso itself drives us to make this alteration, and so our interpretation of the Proviso must reflect the fact that it requires us to change the rules of access to apples, i.e., to restrict access to apples.

Specifically, to appropriate land is to restrict access to apples. And restricted access to apples tends (somewhat paradoxically) to be a precondition of their ongoing availability. To satisfy the

Proviso with respect to apples, one must appropriate *land*, not apples. Hence, land appropriation is not a violation of the Proviso (given that the Proviso applies first and foremost to food) under those circumstances, but must instead be required by it. I say more about the Proviso with respect to land at the end of the next section.

Preserving Resources for Future Generations

Two assumptions I made in deriving this conclusion are worth discussing. First, I interpret the Proviso's requirement that enough and as good be left for others as referring to future generations as well as to the present one. As Sanders (1987, p. 377) puts it: "What possible argument could at the same time require that the present generation have scruples about leaving enough for one another, while shrugging off such concern for future generations?"

Locke thought the point of property was that it helped preserve the human race, which he undoubtedly meant to include future generations. This does not mean Locke also intended the Proviso's reference to "others" to be about future generations, but the suggestion is surely a strong one. Moreover, if Locke did not think of the Proviso as protecting future generations, he should have, and so should we. If we aspire to preserve humankind, leaving something for our own generation is not enough. The land must be saved for future generations too. As scarcity rears its ugly head, a given generation's preservation of the land for future generations discharges its obligation to satisfy the Proviso in the only way that matters in the long run. And if we (latecomers ourselves, after all) do not leave resources for the next generation, we must, somewhere along the line, be failing to leave resources for others, whether or not we read 'others' as being *defined* in terms of future generations.

This is why I have insisted that the Proviso not only permits original appropriation (which is a significant point in itself) but actually requires it. One might suppose that the Proviso does not literally require original appropriation, because we would surely satisfy the Proviso were we simply to lie down and die. Perhaps this is right, but if the intent of the Proviso is to regulate original appropriation in such a way as to facilitate the human race's preservation, then obeying it by simply dying misses the Proviso's point.

That is not to say members of the first generation will not, sometimes rightly, feel disadvantaged by appropriations of their contemporaries (perhaps even to the point of wishing their contemporaries would lie down and die). Nevertheless, she who removes the first plot of land from the commons is doing something the Proviso requires to be done by somebody (because, again, trees left in common are subject to ruinous overuse by those who do not care—or who cannot afford to care, given the logic of the commons—about leaving enough and as good for others). If someone objects that he would rather have met that requirement himself, Jane can answer, "You're objecting to my doing something that had to be done by someone. I was in a position to pick who was going to do it, and I picked me. You would have picked you, which would have been similarly unobjectionable. But that isn't how it happened."

He might well respond that he is not objecting to her act of appropriation, but rather to the way she distributed what she appropriated, or the fruits thereof.[4] Perhaps his argument is sound, but in any event, because his objection is not against the removal as such, we have no quarrel with him here. He concedes our point that people must acquire goods to be able to save them for future generations. We concede his point that once one acquires goods, there are limits on what one can do with them. For present purposes, we leave open the possibility that among such limits are those pertaining to redistribution.

Moreover, if population pressure is already severe enough to limit relative latecomers' opportunities even in the first generation, that means population pressure will limit their opportunities whether or not appropriation is allowed. (And if needing to make fence posts for a living is a disappointment, foraging the commons elbow to elbow would be so much the worse.) Whether or not appropriation is allowed, those who come relatively late all find themselves in the same position, whatever generation they belong to: Either the land has already been appropriated, or any that has not been cannot be—and is probably on the way to ruin. But when some of the land has been appropriated, at least relative latecomers can hope to secure the opportunity to acquire unruined land from previous owners, or at least to exchange their labor for a share of what the land can produce. Those who appropriate land can see to it that something is left for the future by assuming responsibility for the land, which means assuming the right to prevent those who would overuse it from doing so. Those who merely appropriate apples perform no such service.

The Proviso, it should be noted, is a principle of justice pertaining to original acquisition, not to rectifying past injustice. The original situation is not fair, and appropriating land does not thereby make it fair. On the other hand, *not* appropriating land does not make the situation fair either. Those who show up late in the race to appropriate land typically have little reason to suppose they would have done better by showing up similarly late in a race to appropriate apples from the commons. On the contrary, because the prizes tend to be so much smaller in the commons, latecomers typically would do that much worse. That they have shown up late through no fault of their own is something to consider when distributing prizes. But that they find themselves late in a race for land rather than late in a race for apples is something for which they should simply be thankful.

My second assumption concerns exactly what it is that must be left for future generations. As our story goes, protecting Group II's interests requires not that apples or trees or land be left in common for Group II to build fences around, but that the source of apples be preserved so that Group II will have something to eat. And it is a good thing that apple trees need not be left in common for Group II—when a scarce good is left in the commons, it will be overused. To ensure that something worth having will be left for Group II, someone in the first group has to build fences.

My second assumption, then, is that what future generations need is resources to *use*. They do not need to acquire resources through initial appropriation. Again, this seems to be Locke's intention,[5] but more importantly, it should be ours as well. Latecomers arrive too late to hope to acquire valuable land by original appropriation.

If what is important is leaving resources for use, then leaving resources for original appropriation is not necessary. Thus, leaving land in the commons is not necessary. In fact, it is imperative not to leave land in the commons, given what will happen to it there. Sooner or later, the only land worth having will be previously appropriated land. Therefore, the Proviso cannot be read as mandating the preservation of opportunities for initial acquisition.

Because appropriation of land inevitably leaves less land in common for others to appropriate, one naturally presumes that it likewise inevitably violates the Proviso with respect to *land*. To satisfy the Proviso with respect to *apples*, one has no choice but to violate the Proviso with respect to land—or so one might conclude. Carol Rose, for instance, says: "To be sure, *any* appropriation diminishes to some tiny degree the amount of a resource that is available to others" (1987, p. 426). But although Rose's point appears to be obvious, it is nevertheless incorrect. It is not true that appropriation of land inevitably decreases the amount of land available to others. It only inevitably decreases what is available for *original appropriation* by others, which is not the same thing at all.[6] Thus, appropriation of land is not only required by the Proviso with respect to apples but is also permitted by the Proviso with respect to land.

The Status of Contemporary Holdings

Thomas Mautner (1982, pp. 267-269) argues that theories of original appropriation have no contemporary relevance. Why not? Because even if we produce a workable criterion of fair original appropriation, legitimizing contemporary land holdings would still involve showing that they were acquired in accordance with that criterion. But as a matter of fact, the histories of contemporary holdings are generally laced with episodes of force and fraud. (Nor does Mautner think a theory of original appropriation would help in deciding how to *rectify* historical injustices, and I follow him in this respect.)

Mautner's point is well taken, but my admittedly idiosyncratic reading of the Proviso has a contemporary relevance that Mautner did not anticipate. First, an obvious point: Even today, many resources are still largely held in common. To give one example, the coral reefs of the Philippine and Tongan islands are currently being ravaged by destructive fishing techniques. Where fishermen once used lures and traps, they now pour bleach (i.e., sodium hypochlorite) into the reefs. Partially asphyxiated, the fish float to the surface and become easy prey. Unfortunately, the coral itself suffocates along with the fish, and the dead reef ceases to be a viable habitat. ("Blast-fishing," also widely practiced, consists of using dynamite rather than bleach.) What goes through the minds of these fisherman as they reduce some of the most beautiful habitats in the world to rubble? Perhaps some of them think, quite correctly, that if they do not destroy a given reef, it will shortly be destroyed by someone else, so they might as well be the ones to catch the fish. Various groups are trying to save the reefs by effectively removing them from the commons, making other groups very angry in the process. (See Gomez, et al., 1981 and Chesher, 1985.) The issue of how such appropriation might be justified is of contemporary relevance if anything is. Moreover, my interpretation of the Proviso implies that preserving the ecology of the reefs should be regarded as the pivotal issue, which strikes me as a point in its favor.

Second, and perhaps less obviously, my argument also bears on currently held resources that were appropriated long ago. It does more than show that, despite how things actually worked out, things *could* have worked out in such a way that original appropriation and subsequent history *would* have been legitimate. Justifying original appropriation by no means suffices to justify current holdings, of course, but my justification of original appropriation does have the following critically important implication: One cannot, in blanket fashion, base claims of historical injustice on the a priori argument that current holdings must, after all, have been originally acquired somewhere along the line. On the contrary, claims of historical injustice must refer to the *actual historical records* of particular extant holdings.

Third, my argument suggests that there is a sense in which the Proviso has justificatory significance above and beyond the role it plays as a criterion of just original appropriation. Consider that although removing goods from the commons is necessary if goods are to be preserved for future generations, it is not sufficient. Original appropriation by itself does not guarantee that goods will be preserved for future generations. In other words, original appropriation is required to satisfy the Proviso, and this fact suffices to justify original appropriation. But it does not suffice to justify any and all the ways in which one's holdings might be *used*.

This suggests that holdings may satisfy (or fail to satisfy) the Proviso insofar as it pertains to the use of resources rather than to their initial acquisition. I call this sense of the Proviso the *use-proviso* to stress the change of topic. We have been talking about the emergent justification of property as an outgrowth of legitimate original appropriation. The use-proviso, in contrast, concerns the teleological justification of property as a vehicle for preserving resources for the future. The use-proviso requires that those who appropriate resources also practice, in some sense, ecologically sound management. Satisfying the use-proviso would mean that regardless of what has happened in the past, an owner could claim, as a straightforwardly teleological justification for her holdings, that they are being properly cared for and will still be there for future generations when she dies.

The justificatory weight of the use-proviso (however much it has) may be used to criticize as well as to defend current holdings.[7] For renewable resources, like forests, and generally for resources that can be effectively used without being destroyed, like park land, one ought to leave the land in the same shape it was in when one found it. For resources that cannot be effectively used without destroying them, like oil, this requirement would be too strong. After all, for goods that can be consumed only once, *someone* will eventually have to deal with their already having been depleted. Thus, distant generations cannot have the same claims as proximate ones to nonrenewable resources. At most, they will be able to point out that such resources should be replaced by something as good (and not necessarily the same *kind* of resource).

Of course, this leaves us with the issue of what 'as good' really means, and this issue may be hard to settle. One person might claim, while chopping down redwoods to make room for a hamburger franchise, that he is leaving enough and as good for others, whereas everyone else agrees he is simply spoiling his land. In a similar vein, we might ask, "If a person is not inclined to leave enough and as good for others when in the commons, what is going to make him leave enough and as good when it comes to his own property?" Undoubtedly, a few owners will care so little about the future that they will ruin their own land, despite the loss to themselves of its future value. And some Tongan fishermen, given ownership of a reef, might prefer to destroy its future productivity for the sake of maximizing a one-time harvest, despite the fact that they will then be left with nothing. Nevertheless, this lamentable folly is no reason for the rest of us to give such people the opportunity to ravage everything by leaving it all in the commons. That they ruin their own property is bad enough.

Consider also that in the commons, people have comparatively little incentive to save the land even if they do care about their future. Even those Tongan fishermen who would like to save the reefs for their children continue to dynamite and poison the reefs, because as long as the reefs remain in commons, they do not have the option of choosing between long-run and short-run gains. Rather, their choice is between short-run gains for themselves and short-run gains for whoever shows up next. Exclusive control over a stream of benefits gives us both the means and the motive to maximize that stream's long-run value. Once we lose control over this stream, our incentive is to maximize the immediate value we can extract. (This also holds if the future we care about is the human race's rather than our own. The property we save from ourselves can be preserved by us as we see fit, but the commons we save belongs to everyone and is subject to ruination by others whether or not we save it from ourselves.) When one has control over a parcel of land, its future and one's own are bound together as tightly as possible, and this arrangement makes the most of whatever tendencies one has to care about the future.

Admittedly, fencing the commons is not a panacea. People sometimes ruin their own property. Sometimes an injunction to care for it properly is needed. (How one would acquire the right to issue such injunctions is a separate question, implicitly addressed in Chapter 7.) But this is no reason to regret that the property has been removed from the commons. On the contrary, if the property is controlled by some identifiable party, then at least some identifiable party exists who can be held responsible for it. There is some person or group upon whom the needed injunction can be served.

Summary

A key problem for the liberal theory of property concerns property's emergent justification, specifically the justification of initial acquisition of resources from the common stock. There is a public goods problem in the commons. The problem will destroy the common stock if left unsolved. Original appropriation solves it. Hence, property and other forms of exclusive control can be emergently justified as coming into existence via justified (albeit teleologically justified) original appropriation. My argument does not settle questions of comparison among alternative property institutions, but it does settle that institutions of exclusive control in general are immune to the sweeping objection that the initial acquisition of property cannot be justified by the lights of the Proviso. In establishing this, my argument rebuts an objection that is often leveled against private property, but which applies equally to institutions for establishing exclusive control in general.

If we should leave enough and as good for others, we should above all leave enough and as good for future generations. To leave enough and as good for future generations, we must protect them from present-day commons tragedies. Removing resources from the commons is a means of satisfying the Proviso because what we must preserve for future generations are opportunities to use resources, not opportunities to originally appropriate them. This must be so, because under conditions of scarcity, if we want resources to be there for future generations, leaving resources in the commons for them to remove on their own is out of the question. My interpretation of the Proviso, far from ruling out original appropriation, actually requires it.

Chapters 4 through 6 assume the existence of property institutions. I discuss property's moral limits in Chapter 7, after having developed a picture of how public goods problems bear upon the nature and limits of property's teleological justification. First, however, we consider in Chapter 3 the nature and source of the right to punish that gives the institution of property the bite it needs to serve its purpose.

3

The Right to Punish

The institution of property did not emerge by consent. Neither did government. Many of us tend to find exactly one of these facts troublesome (although we do not agree on which one). I am not sure how to account for this apparent double standard. Perhaps we implicitly dismiss nonconsensual emergence as irrelevant to the *teleological* justification of institutions we like, while holding that nonconsensual emergence is a crucial impediment to the *emergent* justification of institutions we dislike. If so, then explicitly distinguishing between emergent and teleological justification will help us avoid the double standard by making it more obvious. Chapter 2 showed how an institution, namely the institution of property, could be emergently justified despite having emerged by a nonconsensual process (i.e., by original appropriation). This chapter tries to do something similar for the government-run institution of punishment.

The argument in Chapter 2 was based on a principle of original appropriation that was in turn teleologically justified as a solution to a specific public goods problem—the need to avoid the tragedy of the commons. Unfortunately, where we find property, we will also find theft. Rules, some would say, are made to be broken. In any event, it is true that where there are rules, questions arise concerning what is to be done, and by whom, to rule-breakers. How does the state acquire the right to punish (and perchance to deter) thieves and other assorted rule breakers? This chapter discusses institutions devised to punish those who fail to observe the rules of the property institution discussed in Chapter 2.

The philosophy of law takes up perennial questions concerning whether there is a right to punish, what it means, how or why it is that someone ever comes to be legitimately punishable by others, what form punishment may take, and so on (see Schmidtz, 1987b). In keeping with the subject of this book, I pose a question asked less often: Assuming there is a right to punish, why is it the *state*—and only the state—that has this right?

I argue that a state can acquire an exclusive right to punish even if individuals also have a right to punish and even if they do not relinquish that right voluntarily. Thus, this chapter and Chapter 2 set out conditions under which the institutions of property and punishment can be emergently justified despite having arisen without consent. To preface the more general discussion of public goods problems that continues in Chapter 4, I conclude this chapter by discussing Michael Levin's argument that property and punishment are the *only* justifiable political institutions.

The Emergence of the Right to Punish

Do governments have the exclusive right to punish? Or would it require unanimous consent, something no government has, to confer that right? If the exclusive right to punish does not come from the consent of its citizens, where does it come from? I begin with Nozick's account of how the state could acquire the right to punish, because it nicely introduces the concepts that my own account uses as points of departure.

A minimal state is, roughly, one that is limited to providing peace-keeping services such as police protection, national defense, and a court system. In Nozick's invisible-hand story, a minimal state evolves in three stages. In the first stage, a dominant protection agency (DPA) emerges from the Lockean state of nature. Individuals in this state of nature have *first-order* rights, i.e., rights to life, liberty, and property, and the *second-order* right to punish those who violate first-order rights (Nozick, 1974, p. 10). Because protecting oneself from offenders (not to mention punishing them) in a Lockean state of nature is often dangerous or impractical for individuals, people band together to form mutual protection associations. Eventually, some members become protection specialists. Thus, mutual protection associations evolve by division of labor into protection agencies. When disputes occur between protection agencies, clients of agencies that lose disputes tend to transfer their business to agencies that win. Because of this, and also because of constant or increasing economies of scale, one agency eventually dominates its geographical domain. Thus executive power—the power to protect against and to punish rights violators—comes to be centralized.

In the second stage of Nozick's story, the DPA evolves into an ultraminimal state. Not everyone in the DPA's domain relinquishes executive power to the DPA by choice, but the DPA forbids independents to exercise executive power by methods that pose excessive risks to its clients. This prohibition characterizes the ultraminimal state; it creates an ongoing noncontractual relationship.

In the third stage, the ultraminimal state becomes a minimal state. By prohibiting self-help (that is, by prohibiting individual initiative in punishing criminals after the fact), the ultraminimal state puts at least some independents at a disadvantage. Their ability to deter rights violators becomes dependent solely upon their ability to make their possessions and persons at least appear crime-proof before the fact. Yet according to Nozick's *principle of compensation*, reducing general fear by prohibiting unusually risky activities (such as self-help punishment) is justified, provided those who gain from the prohibition compensate those who are put at a disadvantage (Nozick, 1974, p. 83). The ultraminimal state compensates independents by protecting them, and this provision of services to nonclients transforms it into a minimal state.

Thus the state emerges by a process of prohibition plus compensation. By prohibiting self-help, a DPA comes to monopolize the power to enforce rights and punish violators. Crucially, it acquires the *right* to exercise these powers by offering compensatory protection to the disadvantaged (and thereby comes to offer universal protection within its domain). The ultraminimal state thereby becomes a minimal state, allegedly violating no one's rights in the process.[1]

Postema's Challenge

The transition to my account from Nozick's is motivated by Gerald Postema's critique of Nozick, a critique that implicitly challenges most other liberal accounts of the right to punish as well. Postema (1980, pp. 325-328) questions whether the DPA could possibly acquire the kind of right to punish that characterizes states. In the Lockean view, which Postema also attributes to Nozick, the state is essentially an agent. It can have only those rights that individuals have in the state of nature and that it acquires from them by voluntary transfer.

Postema, however, poses the following dilemma for Nozick: The individual's *right* to punish in the state of nature implies that others have correlative obligations not to interfere. However, a *liberty* to punish is a very different matter. A liberty does not imply correlative obligations, which is what distinguishes "mere liberties" from full-blooded rights. If the right to punish implies that others must not interfere, then the DPA violates this right when it interferes—when it does not allow independents to exercise their right to punish. On the other hand, if the so-called right is merely a liberty, the DPA's clients can transfer only mere liberties to the agency, and the sum of these mere liberties remains nothing more than a mere liberty. Either way, therefore, the DPA never gains the genuine right to punish (i.e., a right with which citizens cannot interfere) that, when combined with the power to exercise that right *as* a right, is characteristic of legitimate states. Note that this dilemma is not only a problem for Nozick. Contractarian versions of the emergent approach must also face Postema's objection that the state either breaks its obligation not to interfere with independents or, if no such correlative obligation exists, it never acquires more than a mere liberty itself. In fact, any attempt to justify the right to punish as emerging by consent will run into the dilemma Postema poses.

My first reaction to Postema's challenge was to consider whether we could meet it by abandoning the Lockean story in favor of a Hobbesian account according to which citizens *renounce* the right to punish rather than transfer it to the DPA. If the individual's right to punish is a mere liberty, a prohibition against exercising it will limit individual liberty, to be sure, but will not violate individual rights. This avoids the dilemma's first horn.

To avoid the dilemma's second horn, suppose the DPA begins with its own mere liberty to punish but requires through its service contracts that clients renounce their mere liberty to interfere with the DPA's exercising its liberty. The DPA's right to punish thus *becomes* a genuine right—or at least an approximation thereof—as citizens (i.e., clients) enter such contracts. This transformation occurs because to enter the contract is to renounce the liberty to interfere with the DPA, which is equivalent to accepting the correlative obligation not to interfere with the DPA. When this correlative obligation is conjoined to the DPA's own liberty, the result constitutes a genuine right.

The problem with this approach is that not everyone is subject to the correlative obligation.[2] Independents would retain the mere liberty to interfere with the DPA when it exercised its right to punish. As far as independents are concerned, the state's mere liberty to punish never becomes anything more than that. But this raises questions only about the scope of the emerging state's jurisdiction, not its existence. The DPA in any event has authority over clients insofar as *they* are no longer at liberty to interfere. Perhaps a DPA with jurisdiction of such limited scope cannot properly be thought of as a state. This would certainly be true if independents had the *right* to interfere with the DPA. But we are only supposing here that independents are at liberty to interfere. The DPA in turn is at liberty to prohibit independents from exercising their liberty. According to this approach, its prohibitions do not violate rights.

Moreover, the existence of independents might restrict the scope of the DPA's rightful authority less than one might think, for the DPA can have the right as well as the liberty to prohibit self-help by independents. Why? Because the liberty to punish is intrinsically limited. A second-order mere liberty to punish rights violators could be overridden by the first-order rights of bystanders to life, liberty, and property. For instance, I do not have the right to bomb an apartment building, even if one of its tenants commits a capital offense. The DPA has the right as well as the liberty to prohibit such methods of self-help punishment because independents have neither the right nor even the mere liberty to punish by methods that would subject innocent bystanders, including DPA clients, to unwarranted risks.

How States Acquire the Right to Punish

The previous point, of course, obliges me to explain what it means for a risk to be unwarranted. The attempt to explain this, however, led me to develop an entirely different line of response to the dilemma posed by Postema. I have tried to escape the dilemma by replacing a Lockean fiction about transferring rights with a Hobbesian fiction about renouncing rights. As an alternative response, suppose we reject both fictions. After all, we need to justify the state to ourselves, not to the characters in our story. Is there a more satisfying account of how states, the ones we actually live under, acquired the right to punish? Or if they have no such right, how could they get it?

I claimed that the second-order right to punish can be overridden when exercising it would conflict with first-order rights. At the very least, it seems unlikely that people ever have the right to punish by whatever methods they please. Suppose instead that people (including independents) have the right to practice only the punishment method that poses the least risk to clients (and others) as innocent *bystanders*.[3]

What makes this especially interesting is that with the emergence of government (or a suitably powerful precursor thereof, such as a DPA or a tribal chieftain), relying upon the government may *become* the least risky method available. If the right to punish is, say, something like the second-order right to employ the punishment method that minimizes the likelihood of first-order rights violations, the government can acquire, as if by invisible hand, the sole right to punish. It can do this simply by becoming the least risky vehicle for exercising that right (unless even the least risky vehicle is unacceptably risky; if even the least risky vehicle tended to start nuclear wars, we could argue that no one has the right to punish). Independents, in effect, quite naturally lose the right to practice *self-help* punishment, because self-help is no longer a legitimate means by which to exercise their right to punish. And this change in what counts as legitimately exercising their right to punish can occur *whether or not they consent* to that change.[4] In this respect, they effectively lose their political independence, regardless of whether they or anyone else intended that result.

Of course, working out the details of this theory is no minor task. For example, the least risky method of punishment would, on its face, involve doing nothing, thereby imposing no risks at all. A more sophisticated reading will balance the marginal risk (of first-order rights violations) created by more aggressive methods against the marginal risk created by criminals who otherwise will remain at large. That the existence of unpunished criminals sends the wrong signal to prospective criminals is another risk factor to consider.

At any rate, I hope that puzzles at this level will not obscure the point of my proposal. The point is that we can account for the emergence of the right to punish without having to appeal to hypothetical consent or, for that matter, to hard-to-get actual consent. Nor, I should add, does this account require the assumption that individuals have the natural right to punish. The account works in spite of this assumption, not because of it. (We could replace the assumption that people have the second-order right to punish with, for example, the much weaker assumption that people have no right to practice unnecessarily risky punishment methods.) It explains how the right to punish becomes effectively exclusive *even if* individuals have the right to punish and *even if* individuals do not relinquish it.

Nor, for that matter, does this approach presume that institutions have rights over and above the rights held by individual officeholders. As long as we are supposing there is such a thing as an individual right to punish, we may suppose that officials who administer institutional punishment are exercising the same individual right they had all along—the difference being that (as with everyone else) what counts as exercising their right changed as the institutionalization of punishment took place. For other people, what counts as exercising their right is reliance on the institution, as long as its officers run it sufficiently well. For those running the institution, what counts as exercising their right (i.e., what for them minimizes the likelihood of first-order rights violations) is punishing people in accordance with the institution's rules.

Nor is the prohibition of self-help necessarily paternalistic; it protects citizens not so much by protecting them from themselves as by protecting them from each other. If individuals protest that they have the right to engage in self-help, the state's answer is that (1) they have no right to submit their neighbors to pointless risk and (2) self-help became a typically pointless risk as the state became better at exercising the right to punish on citizens' behalf.

Finally, I presume that some modern states could substantiate such a claim. Hence, the story is more than just an exercise. I am suggesting that if there are actual states that have the right to punish, they got it by becoming much better (in terms of minimizing the risks imposed on innocent bystanders) at exercising that right on behalf of citizens than citizens are at exercising it on their own behalf. On this account, the state can acquire the exclusive right to punish even if citizens have neither granted it that right nor relinquished their own.

This is not how Nozick told the story, to be sure. Nor am I concerned with defending Nozick's version. But my version shows that invisible-hand models have the internal resources to provide a plausible account of the nature and origin of one of the most notable features of legitimate government: the right to punish.

The Right to Impose Risk

I explained in Chapter 1 why the least problematic kind of emergent justification consists of showing that an institution arose by consent. Because we do not observe the requisite sort of consent on a large enough scale to justify the state, however, we have had to consider nonconsensual processes by which states might emerge without violating rights. In this chapter, I have argued that a certain kind of teleological justification of the state's exclusive right to punish can reshape the moral borders around individuals in such a way that the state need not cross them in the process of securing its exclusive right. Thus, the right to punish can be emergently justified as well (at least in the weak sense of rebutting the presumption that its emergence violated rights), even if it does not emerge by consent. The accompanying teleological justification that makes all this possible presumes that the state's punishment method is the method that imposes the least risk on innocent bystanders. (Also presumed, of course, is that individuals do not have the right to employ more risky methods.)

In the law and economics literature, however, there already exists an influential account of the nature of rights that deals very nicely with the problem of how to evaluate actions that impose risks on innocent bystanders. Moreover, this more prominent account seems inconsistent, in an interesting way, with my account of the right to punish. Here, I first describe the more standard account and then explain why rejecting it may be part of the price of accepting mine.

Guido Calabresi and A. Douglas Melamed (1972, pp. 1105ff) distinguish three kinds of protection for property rights:

1. When *property rules* are in force, property cannot be transferred except with the owner's consent.
2. When *inalienability rules* are in force, property cannot be transferred even with consent.
3. When *liability rules* are in force, property can be transferred even without consent if proper compensation is made.

One attractive feature of this scheme, not mentioned by its proponents, is that it seems to explain why you can have a right to your car even though it may be permissible for your neighbor to steal it in a life-and-death emergency. In Chapter 2 (note 1), I analyzed property rights as conjunctions of owners' prerogatives to use property and correlative restrictions on its use by others. (For the most part, however, the analysis of property rights is deferred until Chapter 7.) The Calabresi and Melamed scheme allows us to say that normally the restriction that your property rights impose on others is constituted by a property rule. In a desperate emergency, your property is not protected by property rules, but this does not mean you do not have property rights anymore (and perhaps never really did). It just means that circumstances affect the nature of the restriction (and may or may not also affect the nature of the prerogative).

Transaction costs, within the framework of an economic analysis of law, supply one reason to think legal rights are protected sometimes by liability rules and sometimes by property rules.[5] In emergencies, the cost of not taking your car until you give permission could be someone's life. When the cost of obtaining consent from owners is prohibitively high, liability rules apply. (Calabresi and Melamed emphasize that the rules also might be chosen on the basis of their different implications for wealth distribution.)

On a larger scale, the Calabresi and Melamed scheme also allows us to say something more about the nature of first-order moral rights and risky activities. Unintentional harms can be caused by risky activities. The right not to be unintentionally harmed can be protected by liability rules. If property rules were operative at all times, then risky activity would require prior negotiation with everyone subject to the risk, which would effectively preclude the operation of automobiles, among other things. The transaction costs would be insuperable. But if your right is protected only by a liability rule, this suggests that as long as others are willing to compensate you for any damages, they may go on practicing risky activities, including self-help punishment.

The trouble, at least from my point of view, is that Calabresi and Melamed's account may be inconsistent with my explanation of how the state acquires the exclusive right to punish. By their account, people apparently would not lose the right to engage in self-help when self-help becomes unnecessarily risky compared with emerging alternatives. Rather, the right not to be subjected to the risks of others' self-help would be protected by a liability rule. The state would be justified in requiring compensation but not in prohibiting self-help altogether.

There are two ways to respond to this possibility. First, we might say that although the right not to be subjected to risk is generally protected by a liability rule, the right not to be subjected to *pointless* risk (such as the risk imposed by drunken drivers) must still be regarded as being protected by property rules. Besides being intuitively plausible, this rules out subjecting innocent bystanders to the pointless risks of self-help punishment. (And the risks become pointless if and when safer methods become available.) Responding in this manner allows us to retain what is important about my account of the right to punish without sacrificing the Calabresi and Melamed scheme.

A second response involves reconsidering the whole idea of a right not to be subjected to risk. Consider how implausible such a rights claim sounds. To avoid endorsing the preposterously high transaction costs with which this alleged right would saddle us, Calabresi and Melamed propose that rights are not always protected by property rules. A contrasting view is that there is no such thing as a right not to be subjected to risk. That is, although there is presumably a right not to be killed, there is no such thing as a right not to be in danger of being unintentionally killed, and the fact that people do not have such a right explains why we do not need to get their permission every time we create a minuscule risk of unintentionally killing them.

Under this second view, the real question is this: When do we have the right to *impose* risk? Under this view, the operation of cars, for example, concerns the rights (and liabilities) of the driver rather than the rights of all persons other than the driver. Even if one has teleological grounds for claiming the right to engage in a certain kind of activity, one will not have teleological grounds for imposing risks on innocent bystanders beyond those risks that are, for all practical purposes, a necessary part of engaging in the activity. Driving cars and punishing people have in common the fact that they impose risks on the innocent. Therefore, questions about when one has the right to drive and when one has the right to punish must in part be questions about when one has the right to impose risk. Setting aside cases where bargainers agree to accept the risks they impose on each other and thereby emergently justify the right to impose those risks, the right to impose risk is teleologically grounded—when it is grounded at all. Thus, it allows one to do what is necessary to drive cars, punish criminals, and so on, but it cannot allow one to impose pointless risks, such as those imposed on bystanders by drunken drivers. At some point, in assessing whether a given purpose can justify imposing the attendant risks, we still have to perform some kind of risk-benefit calculation. But such a calculation seems less daunting than having to figure out (as the Calabresi and Melamed account requires) when transaction costs become so high that other people's right to be free of risk ceases to be protected by property rules and somehow comes to be protected by liability rules instead.

We should note that supplying a teleological grounding of rights is not the same as supplying conditions under which utility overrides rights. We might try to teleologically ground the right to drive a car, for example, by saying that driving is a sufficiently safe and effective method of getting from point A to point B. It would be apparent from such a teleological grounding, however, that people do not have the right to drive while drunk or to drive at night without headlights, for such methods of getting from point A to point B are unacceptably and unnecessarily risky to innocent bystanders. Thus, to explain why certain ways of driving a car do not count as legitimate ways to exercise the right to drive a car, we can look at the nature of the right itself. We do not have to speak of utility overriding the right to drive a car when one is drunk or when one's headlights do not work.

Similarly, to say the right to punish is not absolute is not to say that its limits are defined by considerations of utility. There are limits to what the right to punish gives one the prerogative to do, but I have characterized these limits by saying, in effect, that what counts as exercising the right to punish is contingent on available alternatives. When options safer for innocent bystanders emerge, an alternative more dangerous to them can no longer count as exercising the right to punish. We should also note that the right to punish is by no means unique in this respect. Indeed, when cars that are safer for innocent bystanders emerge, we can make the same sort of argument about driving more dangerous ones.[6]

Public Goods Provision: Transition to the General Case

In the remainder of this chapter, we consider how my strategies for justifying the particular institutions of property and punishment might be used to justify public goods producing institutions in general. Subsequent chapters build on Chapters 2 and 3 in two ways: They presume the existence of state-enforced property conventions and they continue the general project of justifying institutionalized public goods production.

For citizens, to eschew self-help and thus leave punishment up to political institutions helps provide the public good of peace. For officials, running the institutions helps provide the same good. (Needless to say, concentrations of power invite abuse, an issue I table until Chapter 5.) Thus, minimizing the risk of first-order rights violations is in itself a kind of teleological justification. That an institution is teleologically justified does not entail that it is emergently justified; nevertheless, my account of the right to punish shows that a state need not violate rights when securing the de facto exclusive right to punish. That a state fails to secure consent along the way does not entail that it cannot be emergently justified, for there are nonconsensual processes by which the borders of individual rights might be reshaped so as to allow states (and individuals, as discussed in Chapter 2) to get on with their business without crossing those borders. The process of becoming the safest vehicle for exercising the right to punish is one example of such a process.

According to the story told here, the state's right to punish turns on how the state functions in comparison with the alternative of self-help. To satisfy this criterion of teleological justification, a state would not need to evolve out of a state of nature by way of a DPA (or, for that matter, by an invisible-hand process of any kind) in order to have the exclusive right to punish. The essence of the story was simply that even if individuals do have a right to punish, they do not have a right to impose unnecessary risks on innocent bystanders, and thus relying on the state can become the only permissible means of exercising their right. I am not, however, proposing that state punishment institutions are justified merely because I told a story. Rather, a state's punishment institution is justified insofar as, in its particular case, the essence of the story is true.

The story also shows that the state's exclusive right to punish is consistent with individuals having a second-order right to punish, as long as their right does not include the right to unnecessarily risk violating first-order rights. Thus, governments can emerge in ways that transform the practical scope of individual rights because changes in what the state is justified—teleologically justified—in doing for people can in turn change what people are justified in doing for themselves. These changes make it possible for the state to emerge as an authority over citizens, whether or not citizens consent to this change of status. At the least, changes in the scope of individual rights can shrink the category of persons whose consent is required.

Admittedly, this category could shrink without actually becoming empty. Suppose there exist characters like those portrayed by the actor Charles Bronson; they can terrorize evildoers without any risk to the innocent. When such people engage in self-help, everyone is made safer (except, of course, evildoers). May the state prohibit them from engaging in self-help? Most Charles Bronson fans, I suspect, would say no. But maybe the risk of encouraging people who only *think* they are Charles Bronson types would be far worse than the risk of a blanket prohibition. Still, although this would justify the blanket prohibition from the state's point of view, would it be enough to obligate genuine Charles Bronson types to obey the prohibition? I am not sure, but I think it would at least obligate those who do not know enough to be reasonably sure they really are Charles Bronson types—and that probably includes everyone.

Peace as a Public Good

One might think that the institution of private property and the executive and judicial institutions necessary to protect property rights (broadly defined to include rights to life and liberty) jointly exhaust the category of goods whose provision the state should seek to ensure. Michael Levin takes this position in the course of attempting to derive Nozickian conclusions about the minimal state, an attempt he advertises as not relying on Nozick's premises about natural rights (Levin, 1982, p. 338).

Levin says that people would find it rational to surrender to the state the "sword" (a metaphor for the right to engage in self-help punishment and perhaps also to engage in preemptive first strikes as a means of self-protection) but not the "plow" (a metaphor for the means of producing private goods such as food).[7] Levin says "this crucial difference is supplied by a multiplier effect unique to the problem of war" (1982, p. 348). The multiplier effect works in this way: "My need for my sword and my incentive for keeping it are constituted by my beliefs about your beliefs and intentions. If you did not think you might need your sword against me, I would not need my sword against you" (1982, p. 345). The reason this process of gradually eliminating the need for self-help punishment is called a multiplier effect is that the process feeds on itself. Suppose I know that the government that has undertaken my protection has only a marginal advantage over you if you should decide to attack me. Levin says: "Even knowing this, I relax a little and, seeing me relax, you relax. Seeing you relax, I relax more, and so on. This multiplied effect means I am more secure even though I am less able to defend myself" (1982, p. 347). In other words, as the state becomes willing and able to protect us, I can reduce my weapons budget a bit and still maintain a credible defensive posture. As I reduce my weapons budget, I become less of a threat to you, with the effect that you can decrease your spending even more. In response, I could lower mine a bit more, and hence, so could you, and so on. Thus, Levin concludes: "If I feel safer, you will feel safer from a preemptive attack by me, and I will actually *be* safer (from a preemptive attack by you) because I *feel* safer" (1982, p. 348). The multiplier effect, then, is one account of how relying on the state could become safer for innocent bystanders than self-help punishment.[8]

Is there any similar rationale for the state to deny its citizens the liberty to use their plows? (Or, in contractarian terms, would people have reason to bargain this right away?) Levin says no, because the only way the state can keep its promise to produce food "is to permit or command us to do the very harvesting we would have done had we never made the more extensive bargain." Thus, although the multiplier effect gives us reason to turn to the state to protect us from each other, it cannot provide us with food—or anything other than protection from violence.

The multiplier effect is an interesting idea.[9] Moreover, the phenomenon of "cold war" suggests that the multiplier effect is real—at very least, it works in the opposite direction. (I.e., as a country increases its weapons budget, another country feels less safe and increases its weapons budget, and so on, until eventually each country really is less safe.) Perhaps the multiplier effect also works in the direction hypothesized by Levin; I see no reason to think otherwise. Even so, however, I do not think the multiplier effect grounds the conclusion that bargainers would consent to a minimal state (and no more). Nor do I think it grounds the more straightforward teleological justification of the minimal state implicit in this hypothetical consent argument. (A more straightforward teleological approach would argue that government is good at protecting us from each other but not very good at doing anything else.) To see why, consider that protection from violence is a basket of goods, not a single item. Markets can provide some of these goods (such as security guards for neighborhood defense) and perhaps cannot adequately provide others (such as armed forces for national defense).

Recognizing that protection from violence is a basket of goods will help us to see that the multiplier effect is not necessary to teleologically justify (or to induce people to consent to) state involvement in the protection business. Here is why: One aspect of such protection, namely national defense, involves creating and deploying arms rather than surrendering them. Thus, state involvement in providing national defense is not motivated by the multiplier effect. Yet, if Hobbesian bargainers delegate any task to the state, it is likely to be national defense, despite the absence of the multiplier effect.

Nor is the multiplier effect sufficient to teleologically justify (or to induce people to consent to) state provision of protection. The multiplier effect is manifestly a feature of neighborhood defense (I would put my sword away if only my neighbors would stop carrying theirs), yet my house might be better defended if I hired a security guard with that part of my weapons budget rather than surrender it to the state. If a few of my neighbors used part of their weapons budgets to hire the same guard to include their houses on his or her rounds, the price each of us would have to pay would fall. We would also become less dangerous to each other if we were to spend our money on a commonly held guard rather than upon individually held swords. Thus we would capture the benefits of the existing multiplier effects without a Leviathan.

Therefore, because the multiplier effect is neither sufficient nor necessary to induce consent, other considerations must be posited to explain how the full apparatus of the minimal state would emerge. This suggests that the considerations sufficient to generate the full apparatus of a minimal state might also generate additional state functions regardless of whether the multiplier effect is "unique to the problem of war." The next issue is what these other considerations might be.

If peace would be (as Hobbes assumed) a seriously undersupplied good in the state of nature, then bargainers might rationally create a Leviathan to preserve the peace. Peace might be undersupplied in the state of nature because the peace produced by surrendering the sword is a *public* good. Such peace is a public good because although the benefits generated if and when I drop my sword may far outweigh the costs, the unfortunate fact is that I bear all of the costs, while the benefits are bestowed upon the public at large. At best, I receive only a fraction. That is why I do not drop my sword, despite the fact that we would all be much happier if we all did so.

To use the terminology developed by game theorists (e.g., Luce and Raiffa, 1957), if other people *defect* (i.e., hang on to their swords or sword budgets in this case), then the individual has no reason to *cooperate* (i.e., surrender his own sword or sword budget in this case). The individual is better off defecting, even if other people cooperate. Thus, although mutual cooperation is best for the group, the individual gains more by defecting than by cooperating, no matter what anyone else does. This incentive structure can cause public goods such as national defense to be undersupplied by the market, and this undersupply can lead bargainers to consider creating Leviathan as a nonmarket provider of national defense.

In contrast, to throw our plows onto a pile is to relinquish our means of producing a private good, and nothing more. Throwing plows onto a pile is thus not a productive act, whereas throwing swords onto a pile is, for the very act produces the public good of peace.

But there are things in the world other than plows and swords. For instance, we are all fond of clean air. Surrendering our liberty to burn leaded gasoline would produce a public good, assuming that better alternatives are available (better, that is, in terms of serving the purpose of gasoline without imposing needless risks on innocent bystanders). People engage in both avoidable violence and avoidable pollution because doing so maximizes their expected payoff. In both cases, everyone would be better off if each person individually stopped defecting, but an individual can only lose by doing so *unilaterally*.

This is where the state comes in. With both the liberty to be violent and other kinds of liberty to adopt noncooperative strategies (i.e., defect), a mutual relinquishing of the liberty to defect results in mutual gain, as compared with the payoffs of mutual defection. If we all (freely or otherwise) surrender our swords, then as Levin says, "we expect fighting to stop" (1982, p. 344), and we will no longer need swords to protect ourselves. The state's purpose is to ensure that this relinquishing of liberty is effectively enforced.

We now move to the general case. If we all turn over our liberty to defect, then we expect defecting to stop, and we will no longer need to defect (or to retain the liberty to defect) in order to avoid being victimized by the defection of others. Contrary to Roland Pennock, a critic of Levin, it is not so much that "one could increase his or her ability to satisfy certain basic needs by surrendering the ability to pursue them individually" (Pennock, 1984, p. 261). Rather, in the case of public goods, contractors might increase their ability to satisfy certain needs by (jointly) surrendering the *liberty to refuse* to pursue those needs.

Levin claims that a Hobbesian bargainer "will transfer only his liberty to pursue activities the need for whose pursuit tends to vanish through the act of transfer" (1982, p. 349). The Hobbesian bargainers might indeed transfer to the state their means of protecting themselves against violence-related losses. Oddly, Levin thinks self-defense is the only activity that fits this description, but a contractor's need to protect himself against other kinds of defection-related losses would also vanish through the act of transfer if he and everyone else surrendered their means of protecting themselves against such losses, namely their own liberty to defect.

If rational bargainers would contract with the state to protect them from violence, they might also, for the same reasons, consent to state provision of other public goods. If the latter occurs, contractors will have consented to a more than minimal state. This conclusion in no way assumes that bargainers hold the mistaken (in Levin's opinion, as well as mine) belief that the purpose of a state is to "do for them what they would otherwise have done or attempted to do for themselves" (Levin, 1982, p. 351). Rather, the point is that bargainers would see that without a state, they might not provide—they might not even *attempt* to provide—themselves with certain public goods.

Beyond the Minimal State

Thus, reasons to "throw our swords onto a pile" suggest reasons to relinquish other liberties as well. In the broadest terms, the underlying presumption of the public goods argument is that the purpose of government is to internalize externalities, for it is the mishandling of externalities by the market that, more than anything else, creates a need for government in the first place. To "internalize" externalities is to give agents the incentive to take the full costs and benefits of their actions into account. So, for example, the state might place a surcharge on the purchase of leaded gasoline so that the price paid by motorists more accurately reflects the costs or risks imposed on innocent bystanders by the burning of leaded gasoline.

There is no fundamental difference, at least not at this level of abstraction, between a state's taking steps to regulate pollution and its taking steps to regulate theft. In the latter case, the government must decide how to define theft, how to frame the laws against it, how to enforce those laws, and how much to spend on enforcement mechanisms. The process invites all sorts of inefficiency, but few people think that government should not engage in it.

We could respond to theft by simply letting social pressure, individual conscience, and market responses to demand for anticrime devices handle the problem. The approach we actually take, however, is to forbid theft entirely. Perhaps pollution would be better controlled by turning to tort law or by simply letting groups of concerned citizens educate would-be polluters and their would-be customers or constituents. Nevertheless, outright prohibition, from a moral standpoint, is as viable an option in some cases as is outright prohibition of theft. And from a practical standpoint, for every problem with the prohibition of pollution, there is an analogous problem with the prohibition of theft. This is not to say that the problems carry the same weight in both cases—only that the problems are the same in kind. Someone must decide what levels of negative externality (associated with pollution and theft) are tolerable and then decide how best to spend any funds that might be available for education and law enforcement so as to bring incidence levels within the limits of tolerance. (A certain level of pollution will be tolerated as the price of industry, of course. Likewise, a certain incidence of theft will be grudgingly accepted as the price of producing transferable goods.)

Summary

The account offered here of the right to punish gives an example of how rights could be transferred from individuals to governments without individual consent but at the same time without violating individual rights. More generally, it shows (like the argument of Chapter 2) how there can be such a thing as an emergent justification that does not rely on consent. The account of the state's right to punish does not assume that citizens agree to allow the state to have this right. The account allows for (but does not depend on) the possibility that individual citizens have their own right to punish. It also allows (but does not assume) that institutions per se have rights over and above those of the individuals who run them. Further, the account developed here is not intended to be hypothetical. It is intended as a criterion by which to judge whether actual states have the exclusive right to punish, and it is a standard that we could reasonably demand they live up to.

The tragedy of the commons is a particular kind of public goods problem, a problem of getting people to do their share of the work in preserving resources for the future. Part of the solution to the problem involves institutions of property in particular and exclusive control in general. Another part of the solution is to develop institutions for enforcing property rights and for punishing those who violate them. But the public goods problem comes in other guises. Doing what it takes to avoid a tragedy of the commons in land and other divisible resources is not enough to solve the problem in all its forms. To this more general problem we now turn. The next chapter shows how markets can solve the Prisoner's Dilemma and any public goods problem that can be modeled as one.

4

The Prisoner's Dilemma

What gives governments the right to pay for national defense by taxing citizens? The usual answer is that providing national defense is very important and there is no other way to raise the necessary funds except by taxation. As Mancur Olson puts it, "It would obviously not be feasible, if indeed it were possible, to deny the protection provided by the military services, the police, and the courts to those who did not voluntarily pay their share of the costs of government, and taxation is accordingly necessary" (1965, p. 14). The thrust of the argument is that coercive provision of public goods is teleologically justified. (For lack of a better term, I will use 'coercion' to refer to the initiation of force that is not emergently justified by actual consent. This characterization captures at least part of what is intrinsically objectionable about coercion, but it does so without prejudicing the issue of whether coercion, objectionable though it may be, is sometimes teleologically justified.)[1] But why cannot funds for national defense be raised by voluntary means? Because, many economists and political philosophers would say, national defense is a public good.

A collective good is a good characterized by *nonrivalry in consumption* (i.e., its use by one person does not interfere with its use by others). A public good is a collective good the consumption of which is *nonexclusive* (i.e., if the good is available to one person, it will be available to all, including those who do not help to produce it; see Head, 1962, pp. 197-221). Many activities of existing states can be viewed as attempts to provide public goods. Consider national defense. One citizen enjoying the protection of a national defense system does not reduce the amount of protection enjoyed by other citizens; national defense therefore exhibits nonrivalry in consumption. Further, a nation that defends itself from invasion will be defending those citizens who do nothing to help as well as those citizens who do help, and this feature makes national defense nonexclusive as well. The benefits of government attempts to protect the environment are also essentially nonrivalrous and nonexclusive. That is, my neighbors can enjoy the benefits of clean air without reducing the benefits that I can extract from the same goods. Moreover, they can enjoy these benefits whether or not they help to pay for it.[2] Other goods that are arguably public to varying degrees are police protection, road construction and maintenance, communicable disease research, and so on. (See Mueller, 1979, p. 13 and Shand, 1984, p. 99.) Still other activities, such as the provision of patent and copyright protection, are intended to help privatize (and thus encourage production of) what otherwise would be public goods. (For a superior discussion and critique of intellectual property rights, see Palmer, 1989.)

The government can certainly produce public goods by force, but is force necessary? It might be, and there are two reasons why. First, if the good is nonexclusive, an individual may feel that enough other people will cooperate to produce the good without her help. Hence, the individual may decide not to contribute, because she can enjoy the good for free. I shall call this the *free rider problem* (a commonplace term, but not everyone uses it in precisely this way). A second reason not to contribute arises if a person believes it would be futile to contribute because the good will not be provided anyway. Unless the person receives reasonable assurance that other people will contribute enough to ensure that his own contribution will not be wasted on a hopelessly underfunded cause, the person may decide to save his money. This is an *assurance problem*.[3] This part of the problem does not presuppose that rational agents are self-interested. (For that matter, the free rider problem does not presuppose that rational agents are strictly self-interested.) Allen Buchanan (1985, pp. 72ff) explains nicely how even thoroughgoing altruists can be stymied by a lack of assurance that their contributions will be put to good use.

I propose to solve the assurance problem by means of what I call an assurance contract. Later sections explore this concept in more detail, but the idea, briefly stated, is that via an assurance contract, would-be patrons pledge support to a public goods project. Each pledge becomes enforceable if and only if the total amount pledged to the project is sufficient to make the project viable. If this level of support is not secured within a specified time, would-be patrons contribute nothing. Contributors are thus assured that their money will be spent only if the project promises a return sufficient to make their contributions worthwhile.

I also consider the free rider problem. There are cases in which the free rider problem does not arise and other cases in which using modified assurance contracts can reduce its severity. In particular, the Prisoner's Dilemma (explained in the next section) has a theoretical solution. I then demonstrate that to the extent public goods problems conform to the Prisoner's Dilemma model, the institution of assurance contracts can be teleologically as well as emergently justified. The point of the demonstration is partly to show how public goods problems can be solved, but also partly to illustrate the shortcomings of the Prisoner's Dilemma as a model of the public goods problem. This chapter considers how public goods problems can be solved, insofar as we can model them as Prisoner's Dilemmas. Chapter 5 then considers how our picture of the public goods problem changes, both strategically and morally, if we abandon the Prisoner's Dilemma model.

The Prisoner's Dilemma Model

Given that many public goods are highly desirable, how are they to be produced? How, for example, might the upgrading of road surfaces be financed in an existing residential neighborhood? The cost of producing such goods relative to the benefits derived by any one individual is often so high that people have neither the incentive nor the means to produce them individually. Thus, the production of public goods is often impossible without a cost-sharing arrangement.

The predicament people face when trying to produce public goods by collective action has been modeled by a game called the Prisoner's Dilemma. (See Luce and Raiffa, 1957, pp. 94-102 or Russell Hardin, 1982, pp. 22-30.) In fact, Hardin (p. 25) goes so far as to say that "the problem of collective action and the Prisoner's Dilemma are essentially the same." The following situation illustrates the nature of the game: Suppose you and a confederate—Jane is her name—are about to stand trial for a crime. You must decide whether to keep silent or to turn state's evidence against Jane. Jane faces the same choice. You receive the following offer from the district attorney: In the event that Jane keeps silent, then you will go free if you testify but will receive a one-year sentence if you keep silent; in the event that Jane decides to testify against you, then you will get nine years if you testify but ten years if you keep silent. You must make your choice knowing that Jane has been offered a similar deal.

The information is clearer when put in the form of a matrix. Figure 4.1 shows how Jane will fare depending on the strategies you and Jane select. The upper left quadrant, for instance, shows that if both you and Jane testify, Jane receives nine years. The lower left quadrant shows that if Jane keeps silent and you testify, Jane receives ten years.

Figure 4.1
Prisoner's Dilemma: Payoffs for Jane

		You	
		Testify	Keep Silent
Jane	Testify	9 yr	0
	Keep Silent	10 yr	1 yr

Figure 4.2 is the same as Figure 4.1 except that your payoffs are also given for each possible combination of strategies. In Figure 4.2, payoffs to you are shown in each quadrant's top right corner. (Jane's payoffs continue to be shown in the bottom left corner of each quadrant.)

Figure 4.2
Prisoner's Dilemma

		You: Testify	You: Keep Silent
Jane	Testify	9yr (You) / 9 yr (Jane)	10yr (You) / 0 (Jane)
	Keep Silent	0 (You) / 10 yr (Jane)	1yr (You) / 1 yr (Jane)

Figure 4.2 shows that if you both testify, Jane receives nine years, as already mentioned, and you also receives nine years. If, as in the upper right quadrant, Jane testifies and you keep silent, then she goes free and you are sentenced to ten years.

Insofar as the length of Jane's prison term is the only thing at stake in this game, her *dominant strategy* is to testify. (A strategy is dominant when it is at least as good as, and sometimes better than, any alternative strategy no matter what anyone else does.) Whatever you do, Jane is better off if she testifies than if she keeps silent. The same is true for you. If each of you acts in your own self-interest, you will each play your dominant strategies—both of you will testify.[4]

The situation depicted in Figure 4.2 is a dilemma because if you both do what is best for yourselves and testify, you will get nine years each, whereas if you each keep silent, you will get only one year each. Individually, each of you has done as well as possible, for if either of you had played differently, given the other's decision to testify, you would have received ten years instead of nine. Nevertheless, if the two of you had somehow been able to keep silent as a group, you would both have been better off.[5]

So goes the standard analysis of the Prisoner's Dilemma. The way I have defined free rider and assurance problems, however, sheds a new light on the dilemma. As defined, these two problems are complementary and essential components of the Prisoner's Dilemma.[6] In effect, they constitute the two "halves" of the Prisoner's Dilemma. That is, from Jane's point of view, the left side of the matrix represents her assurance problem. She may be willing to keep silent so that (assuming you also keep silent) she gets one year instead of nine years. But without assurance that you will also keep silent, keeping silent may get her not *one* year instead of nine, but *ten* years instead of nine. This gap, reflected in the difference between Jane's payoffs in the upper left and lower left quadrants, constitutes an assurance problem. The right side of the matrix, by contrast, represents Jane's temptation to free ride. If you keep silent, then she gets only one year by returning the favor. But there is no need for her to return the favor. In fact, by testifying, she avoids prison entirely. Thus the gap between the payoffs of the upper right and lower right quadrants constitutes a free rider problem.

I also depart from more standard characterizations of the Prisoner's Dilemma insofar as I do not assume that the length of your prison term is the only thing you care about. There may be factors to which you can attach value commensurate with the negative value you attach to your prison term. When such factors exist, they can be incorporated into the matrix so that it more accurately reflected your preference ranking (assuming one wants the matrix to reflect preference rankings). There may also be factors you care about that do not exactly fall under the heading of "value." You might, for instance, believe that "squealing" is simply impermissible under the circumstances; you definitely prefer to lighten your sentence, but you do not consider betraying Jane one of your options. Such a factor could not be represented by the matrix's payoffs, because it does not reduce the attractiveness of testifying so much as it entirely eliminates testifying from your list of options.

One could insist that a proper Prisoner's Dilemma matrix must capture everything that the agents involved care about. Satisfying this requirement would have the advantage that the numbers depicted by the matrix could be taken to entail a preference ranking. I do not impose this requirement because I think it is impractical. It implies that we could never know that agents were actually in a Prisoner's Dilemma unless we knew everything that might conceivably affect their preference rankings. We would have developed a conceptual apparatus for nothing.

I view the numbers in the matrix as representing interests rather than preferences, specifically those interests brought into conflict by the situation at hand. (In other words, the numbers represent the actual stakes—e.g., monetary values or lengths of prison terms—rather than the agents' subjective reactions to those stakes.) This allows us to conclude without any residual uncertainty that the conflict of interests depicted in a matrix such as Figure 4.2 is indeed a Prisoner's Dilemma. We may not be certain that the defendants prefer a nine-year sentence to a ten-year sentence, but we can still conclude without doubt that they are in a Prisoner's Dilemma. And taking the numbers to represent only those interests brought into conflict by their dilemma allows us graciously to admit that agents in such situations may have interests above and beyond their interest in maximizing incomes or minimizing prison terms. (See also Russell Hardin, 1988, p. 38.) On the other hand, when I say individuals prefer withholding to contributing, I will be assuming that their preferences track their interests in the case at hand. This saddles us with a residual uncertainty concerning whether preferences track interests in a given case. But the uncertainty here is produced by reality rather than by our model of reality. Obviously, we cannot always be sure that people will do—or will even want to do—what is in their best interest. Thus, keeping us alert to the realism of this kind of uncertainty is a desirable consequence of interpreting the payoffs in terms of interests. In contrast, the uncertainty we thereby avoid—the issue of whether the situation is a Prisoner's Dilemma at all—is purely an artifact of an impractical theory about what Prisoner's Dilemmas are.

Public Goods Problems As Prisoner's Dilemmas

Suppose that a problem of producing public goods by collective action takes the form of a Prisoner's Dilemma. For instance, suppose Jane is asked to contribute $100 toward research aimed at developing a vaccine for the disease AIDS. (If AIDS has already been cured, the reader may substitute something more current.) The vaccine, once developed, will be made available to everyone. The same request is made of 999 of Jane's neighbors.

The return of Jane's investment to her is the value she will receive from the few additional hours of research that her contribution makes possible. Suppose that this value to her is only one dollar. Her individually rational strategy, then, is to refuse to contribute the $100. But if she does contribute, then not just her but all her neighbors also receive a return from her investment. Suppose that they each receive an average of one dollar in value from her investment. Then her $100 contribution would produce a $1,000 benefit for the group. Nevertheless, her dominant strategy is to withhold her contribution. This example illustrates the general truth that contributing a unit of public good generates benefits for the group in excess of the unit's cost, but the unit's cost exceeds the benefits for the individual who contributes the unit. Each individual in the group is strictly better off withholding than contributing. Because the players of this "game" decide as individuals rather than as a group, individually rational strategies thwart collective efforts to produce public goods. The incentive structure is that of the Prisoner's Dilemma. To present this incentive structure in its most general form, let us define a few symbols as follows:

c = the unit investment that each person is asked to contribute

r = the return to a single individual from a single individual's contribution of c

$R = nr$ in a group of n members

In the AIDS vaccine example, each person in a group of 1,000 is asked to contribute c. Jane's contribution of c produces a return of r for each of n persons, with r in this case being an average of one dollar. Because there is nonrivalry in consumption of *r*, the benefits produced by individual contributions do not need to be split. It follows that there are two ways to interpret *R*, depending on whether we are looking at the sum of the whole group's benefits from a single contribution by Jane, or at Jane's benefits from the sum of everyone's contributions. *R* equals the group's total benefit when a single individual contributes—one contribution producing a one dollar benefit that falls in full measure on each of 1,000 persons in this case. *R* also equals Jane's benefit when everyone contributes—1,000 contributions multiplied by a benefit of one dollar per contribution in this case. The ensuing discussion uses whichever interpretation is pertinent to the summation at issue, but *R* denotes the same number on either interpretation.

The vaccine example is presented in matrix form in Figure 4.3, below. Figure 4.4 shows the generalized incentive structure of public goods production. Of the hundreds of possible combinations of contributing and withholding, Figures 4.3 and 4.4 represent the two extremes. The left side shows Jane's situation if no one else contributes. The right side shows Jane's situation if everyone else contributes. Because the incentives for Jane to play NO rather than YES remain operative between the two extremes, the discussion can be generalized. The complete matrix for the group of 1,000 in the AIDS research problem, for example, would have 1,000 columns. For a given contributor, some column in the middle would represent the number of people who must contribute in order for the contributor in question to break even. Columns to the left of the break-even point would represent the contributor's assurance problem, because if the number of contributors is less than that, the contributor's gain will not cover the cost of his or her contribution. For Jane, who gains a dollar benefit from each contribution, the break even point for a hundred dollar contribution is at column 100, for ninety-nine other contributions combined with her own is just enough to cover the cost of her contribution.

Because there is nonrivalry in consumption of the good, *r* is added to *every* player's return for *each* investment of *c*. Thus, if each player in the group contributes (as in the lower right quadrants of Figures 4.3 and 4.4), each player's net gain will be the total return

R, minus his own contribution of *c*, or *R* - *c*. The return to the group as a whole, formulated in terms of benefits to each member, would be the group size multiplied by *R* - *c*.

If one player withholds and the remaining players contribute (as in the upper right quadrants of Figures 4.3 and 4.4), then the cooperative return is lowered by *r*, i.e., from *R* to *R* - *r*, because one less player is investing *c*. Each player's net gain will be (*R* - *r*) - *c*, except for the withholder, whose net gain will be *R* - *r*, because he saves *c* by not contributing to the project.

Figure 4.3
AIDS Research: Incentive Structure of Traditional Donation Process

		The other 999 contribute?	
		NO	YES
Jane contributes?	NO	0 0	999 - 100 999
	YES	1 1 - 100	1,000 - 100 1,000 - 100

The matrices depict the payoffs per person. In the AIDS research example, mutual cooperation has a payoff for the group *as a whole* of 1,000 - 100 (i.e., *R* - *c*), which each person gets, multiplied by the group size of 1,000.

Figure 4.4
Generalized Incentive Structure of Traditional Donation Process

Rest of the group contribute?

Jane contributes?		NO	YES
	NO	0 / 0	$(R - r) - c$ / $R - r$
	YES	r / $r - c$	$R - c$ / $R - c$

Note that because r is an average, there could be individuals for whom r exceeds c. Securing the cooperation of these individuals would not be a problem. There could also be individuals for whom r is so low that R, their prospective total benefit, is insignificant or even negative. These individuals would be at least as happy if the so-called good was not produced at all. For now, I set aside such cases by making the following two critically important assumptions: For all individuals, R substantially exceeds c, and c exceeds r. The first assumption ensures that producing the good is important. The second assumption ensures that the incentive to withhold will be real. Together, the assumptions that R exceeds c and that c exceeds r are necessary and sufficient to ensure that the generalized collective action problem depicted in Figure 4.4 is a Prisoner's Dilemma, exhibiting both the free rider and assurance problems. (And assuming that the excess of R over c is substantial ensures that the Prisoner's Dilemma problem is important.)

In the Prisoner's Dilemma, players have a dominant strategy, and following it leads to wholesale withholding, which has the paradoxically self-defeating effect of *minimizing* the benefits players secure as a group. If Jane sees this and unilaterally changes strategies, however, she only makes things worse for herself. To avoid the result of mutual withholding, she is willing (if necessary) to give up her free ride and pay her share of the price of mutual contribution. What stops her is her lack of assurance that enough others will follow suit to make her contribution worthwhile.

Assurance Contracts

An assurance contract is a contractual agreement to contribute to a public goods project. The distinguishing features of the contract are that it need not specify either the identities of the other parties involved or the extent of the obligations undertaken by other individuals. It need only specify, for each particular party, what consideration is expected from the other parties involved *as a group*.[7]

The purpose of the contract is to give each party an assurance that his contribution will not be wasted on a public goods project that is financially undersupported. (Prospective contributors may reasonably doubt that a project will have worthwhile results even if its funding target is met, but we concentrate here on the problem of eliciting contributions from those who recognize and accept the project's value.) To provide such an assurance, the contract incorporates a feature similar to a "money-back guarantee": The contract is enforceable against a contractor if and only if the rest of the group agrees to contribute enough to ensure that the project's total funding is sufficient to produce a return R that exceeds the contractor's cost c. Recall that each contractor enjoys R in its entirety because of nonrivalry in consumption. (I assume all contributors contribute the same amount c. Of course, there is no obstacle preventing fundraisers from relaxing this assumption by asking, for instance, for contributions greater than or equal to c, if they judge that by doing so they could raise a larger amount.) The contract assures the individual that if the rest of the group does not agree to contribute enough, the individual contributes nothing. His contribution and his return will both be zero.

In the vaccine example, AIDS research could be funded in the same way that research into muscular dystrophy or lung disease is currently funded. Alternatively, these fundraising campaigns could incorporate the assurance contract. Instead of simply announcing a target of a certain number of millions of dollars, as telethons or door-to-door campaigns usually do, these campaigns could announce a target and also guarantee that pledges will not be collected until and unless the total amount pledged reaches the announced target. (This implies that the target must be set with great care, of course, for if it is set too high, the beneficial incentive properties of setting the target will be more than offset by the risk of not meeting the target at all. I return to this issue in Chapter 6.)

A comparison of Figures 4.3 and 4.5 illustrates the point. Figure 4.5 represents the incentive properties of the AIDS research fundraising campaign that incorporates the assurance contract guarantee; Figure 4.3 illustrates the incentive properties of the traditional donation process. Figure 4.5 shows that the assurance contract solves the assurance problem. Even if Jane unilaterally adopts a cooperative strategy (the situation represented by the lower left quadrant of the matrix), she still does not lose money. The possibility of wholesale withholding by the rest of the group no longer implies a risk of suffering a net cost and thus no longer creates an incentive to withhold.

Figure 4.5
AIDS Research: Incentive Structure of Traditional Donation Process Modified by Contractual Solution of the Assurance Problem

		The other 999 contribute?	
		NO	YES
Jane contributes?	NO	0 0	999 - 100 999
	YES	0 0	1,000 - 100 1,000 - 100

The costs of collecting pledged contributions would have to be taken into account when setting the original fundraising target. This is true with or without assurance contracts, of course. With an assurance contract, however, when a target is not met, the contract is not enforceable. If it is not enforceable, it is not enforced. If it is not enforced, there are no enforcement costs. Of course, a person does need assurance either that other players' pledges will actually be collected or that the person's own contribution will be returned if funds actually collected fail to meet the target.

The general form of this solution to the assurance problem is given in Figure 4.6. (Compare this to Figure 4.4.)

Figure 4.6
Generalized Incentive Structure of Traditional Donation Process Modified by Contractual Solution of the Assurance Problem

		Rest of the group contribute? NO	Rest of the group contribute? YES
Jane contributes?	NO	0 0	$(R - r) - c$ $R - r$
	YES	0 0	$R - c$ $R - c$

Solving the assurance problem, as Figures 4.5 and 4.6 show, does not by itself make contributing c a dominant strategy. The free rider problem remains. Nevertheless, the assurance contract is still an effective method of providing collective goods in several kinds of cases in which free rider problems can be avoided. (In Chapter 5, I discuss cases in which the free rider problem cannot be avoided entirely, but the assurance contract still has its advantages.)

Let me stress that my objective is to show that the assurance contract can be used to provide levels of public goods deemed adequate by the people involved. In the vaccine example, a research team has decided that if one thousand people each contribute $100, then the team can proceed with its research. I am not concerning myself with whether $100,000 would be the optimal level of funding for such a project, but only with whether the assurance contract could be used to raise the $100,000. Nor am I concerned at this point with what problems had to be solved before a means of contractual enforcement could emerge, although I do consider such problems in the next chapter.

Assurance Contracts and Incentives to Cooperate

In this section, I discuss two kinds of cases in which assurance contracts would help solve assurance problems and thus would help fundraisers reach their goals. In the next section, I discuss a third kind of case involving free rider as well as assurance problems, and modify the assurance contract so as to address both assurance and free rider problems.

Assurance Problems in Isolation

Case 1: Assume in this case that for each player, R exceeds c so that each player prefers mutual contribution to mutual withholding and must choose either to contribute c or to withhold c. Second, suppose that in a group collectively capable of producing a certain public good, each player is willing to contribute c given assurance that other players will collectively contribute enough to generate a total return larger than the cost of contributing c.

This willingness to "play fair" may seem mysterious within the context of game theory. After all, in Figures 4.5 and 4.6, the upper right box still has a higher payoff than the lower right box. All other things being equal, each player fares better by withholding. On the other hand, all other things are generally not equal. Just as Figure 4.2 depicted only prison terms, Figures 4.5 and 4.6 depict only the costs of producing and the benefits of consuming public goods. But consuming the final product is only one of the benefits contributors might enjoy as a result of the good's production. When a player contributes c, the level of public good he consumes increases by the increment of the good his contribution produces, that is, r. Yet he may also gain personal satisfaction from being part of the solution to a community problem. He may, in other words, be *group*-interested as well as *self*-interested. (See Margolis, 1982, pp.

36ff.) Similarly, people typically are willing to pay a certain amount for the sake of conferring benefits upon family, friends, or fellow citizens. Purchasing collective goods is one way to confer such benefits. People may also benefit in terms of self-interest through the good will and gratitude of their neighbors (or customers). A player who withholds saves *c*, but the effect upon her conscience or reputation may be more important. (See also Brubaker, 1975, p. 154.) Therein lies the point of offering tax exemptions for charitable activities: By helping the fringe benefits bridge the gap between *c* and *r*, tax exemptions help to make it individually rational to contribute *c*.

When such factors outweigh the difference between *c* and *r* in Jane's case, she will prefer the lower right box to the upper right box, all things considered. Thus, withholding will no longer be a dominant strategy. Figure 4.7 reflects this situation. An *FB* (fringe benefit) factor is added to the payoffs for successful contribution to reflect the considerations just discussed. One might suppose there may also be fringe benefits associated with wasted contributions. But even if Jane does have group interests, wasted contributions will not satisfy them. Of course, if we could assume that there are large enough fringe benefits to wasted contributions, we could assume away the assurance problem as well, but I will not make such an assumption here. I assume instead that *FB* in the lower left box is negligible.[8]

Figure 4.7
Case 1: Traditional Incentive Structure Reflecting Fringe Benefits

Rest of the group contribute?

		NO	YES
Jane contributes?	NO	0 0	$FB + (R - r) - c$ $R - r$
	YES	r $r - c$	$FB + R - c$ $FB + R - c$

Where does the assurance contract fit in? Notice that although withholding is not a dominant strategy in Figure 4.7, neither is contribution. The assurance problem remains, leading Jane to prefer the upper left quadrant to the lower left quadrant. In this case, mutual withholding and mutual contribution are both *Nash equilibria* (Luce and Raiffa, 1957, pp. 106-109), which means that each player has an incentive not to change his strategy *unilaterally*. Mutual withholding is a Nash equilibrium because the payoffs are such that if everyone else withholds, then Jane is better off withholding also. Mutual contribution is also a Nash equilibrium because if everyone else contributes, then Jane fares better by contributing because of the fringe benefits involved. Unlike in the kind of equilibrium that results when dominant strategies exist, a player in a Nash equilibrium might have an incentive to change his strategy if others change theirs.

Thus, a player's best strategy in a Nash equilibrium depends partly upon what others do. Because each member of the rest of the group individually faces the same situation, each player has an incentive not to unilaterally change strategies. Without the assurance contract, therefore, mutual withholding would be a stable outcome (as would mutual contribution) even though withholding is not a dominant strategy.

Now suppose we introduce the assurance contract, thus modifying the outcome in the lower left quadrant. The result is depicted in Figure 4.8. With the assurance contract, the incentive not to change a withholding strategy unilaterally no longer exists. Contribution has become a dominant strategy.

Figure 4.8
Case 1: Contractually Modified Incentive Structure Reflecting Fringe Benefits

		Rest of the group contribute?	
		NO	YES
Jane contributes?	NO	0 0	$FB + (R - r) - c$ $R - r$
	YES	0 0	$FB + R - c$ $FB + R - c$

Case 2: In Case 1, we assumed that group-interest has substantial motivating power. Obviously, this assumption would not always be warranted. If we suppose that *FB* in the vaccine example averages no more than \$20, for instance, then *FB* would seldom and possibly never be large enough to bridge the gap between a fixed *c* of \$100 and an average *r* of \$1.

Accordingly, we now restrict our attention to those cases in which we can assume there are no decisively large fringe benefits. We continue to assume that all players prefer mutual contribution to mutual withholding and that each player must choose either to withhold *c* or contribute *c*. We now also assume that players care only about the operative payoffs of the matrix. (In real-world situations, people generally do care about other things, but it is also true that their other concerns often do not greatly affect their behavior.) Thus, if the upper right box has a higher payoff than the lower right box, withholding remains a dominant strategy even if the assurance problem has been solved.

On the other hand, for collective goods, the lower right box pays the individual more than the upper right box, as depicted in Figure 4.9. This can occur because a number of collective goods are not public goods in the technical sense. They can be produced in such a way that their consumption is exclusive. Examples of such goods include freeways, bridges, parks, garbage collection, and public utilities, among others. The AIDS vaccine in our example is a public good only if the provider elects to to provide the vaccine to people without regard to whether they helped to produce it.[9] Although there may be good reason to distribute the vaccine this way, consider how the incentive properties of this method compare with more exclusive methods.

Figure 4.9
Case 2: Traditional Incentive Structure for Exclusive Goods

		The other 999 contribute?	
		NO	YES
Jane contributes?	NO	0 0	999 - 100 0
	YES	0 1 - 100	1,000 - 100 1,000 - 100

Compare Figure 4.9 with Figure 4.3, which depicted the incentives created when vaccine is to be made available to everyone. Figure 4.9 shows how the payoff of the upper right quadrant changes if the vaccine will be made available only to those who help to finance its production. As we can see, exclusion can reduce the payoff to Jane of the upper right box to zero or near zero. Note that exclusion need not reduce Jane's payoff to zero in order to be effective. Given a solution to the assurance problem, exclusion need only reduce the payoff for free riding by more than $c - r$ (100 - 1 in the vaccine example) in order to make contributing c a dominant strategy. For example, in Figure 4.9, Jane's payoff in the upper right quadrant did not have to be reduced from $999 to zero, but only from $999 to less than $900. In the vaccine example, although free riders would not receive the vaccine, their own risk of contracting the disease would be reduced somewhat if the people around them were immunized; thus their benefits would be greater than zero. Even so, the net benefit of getting immunized might generally swamp the benefit of free riding. When this is achieved, as in Figure 4.9, mutual withholding and mutual contribution are Nash equilibria, as they were in Figures 4.5 and 4.6.

Contrast Figure 4.9 to Figure 4.10. Introducing the assurance contract in Figure 4.10 changes the payoff of the lower left box, thereby converting the situation from one in which contributing and withholding are both Nash equilibria to one in which contribution is a dominant strategy. The net cost to Jane of unilateral contribution has dropped from r - c in Figure 4.9 (or 1 - 100 in the vaccine example) to zero in Figure 4.10. By solving the assurance problem, the assurance contract eliminates the incentive not to contribute to the production of exclusive goods and hence makes contributing c a dominant strategy.

Figure 4.10
Case 2: Contractually Modified Incentive Structure for Exclusive Goods

		Rest of the group contribute?	
		NO	YES
Jane contributes?	NO	0 0	$(R - r) - c$ 0
	YES	0 0	$R - c$ $R - c$

Assurance and Free Rider Problems Together

Case 3: One may concede that the assurance contract is sufficient (and consequently coercion is unnecessary) to correct the assurance problem in the case of goods allowing exclusion. One may also maintain, however, that coercion is needed to produce nonexclusive collective goods, i.e., public goods in the technical sense, because of the free rider problem. From here on, I focus on nonexclusive goods.

In Case 3, we continue to assume that each player prefers mutual contribution to mutual withholding and must choose either to contribute *c* or withhold *c* (and, of course, that *r* is less than *c*). These assumptions define the Prisoner's Dilemma, in which withholding is a strictly dominant strategy. The assumption that everyone prefers mutual contribution to mutual withholding implicitly contains assumptions that people understand their own payoffs and also that there are limits to how spiteful people can be. (They would rather see everyone gain than see no one gain.) Moreover, people prefer mutual contribution to mutual withholding given their cost share *c*, which raises questions about how cost shares are to be assigned in the first place.[10] If we had to depend on cost shares emerging by a process of offer and counteroffer, transaction costs (i.e., costs of the bargaining process itself) could quickly become prohibitive. These implicit assumptions are important and are discussed further in Chapter 5.

Figure 4.11
Case 3: The Prisoner's Dilemma

Rest of the group contribute?

Jane contributes?	NO	YES
NO	0 0	$(R - r) - c$ $R - r$
YES	r $r - c$	$R - c$ $R - c$

Figure 4.11 is a reproduction of figure 4.4. Introducing the assurance contract into the matrix would change the payoffs of the lower left box to zero for each player (as in figure 4.6), but this will not discourage free riding. On the other hand, a modified assurance contract that strictly required pledges from all players in order to become enforceable against any of them would certainly discourage free riding.[11] If unanimous consent is required to make the contract enforceable, then a single withholder invalidates the contract. For each player, the cooperative outcome is impossible without his contribution. Thus, the payoff of the upper right box, where the rest of the group contribute c but Jane withholds, drops to zero. Hence, the lower left and upper right quadrants of the Prisoner's Dilemma matrix effectively collapse into routes to the outcome of the upper left quadrant. In effect, mutual contribution and mutual withholding are the only possible outcomes. Because each player in this case prefers the lower right quadrant, which pays $R - c$, to the other three quadrants, which pay zero, each player will agree to an assurance contract that requires each player to contribute c. Therefore, by making the upper right and lower left quadrants of the Prisoner's Dilemma effectively inaccessible, an assurance contract that requires unanimity makes contribution a dominant strategy in the Prisoner's Dilemma. This solution is shown for the vaccine case in Figure 4.12 and for the general case in Figure 4.13.

Figure 4.12
Case 3: AIDS Research—The Prisoner's Dilemma Solved

The other 999 contribute?

Jane contributes?	NO	YES
NO	0, 0	0, 0
YES	0, 0	1,000 - 100, 1,000 - 100

Figure 4.13
Case 3: The Prisoner's Dilemma—Generalized Contractual Solution

Rest of the group contribute?

Jane contributes?	NO	YES
NO	0, 0	0, 0
YES	0, 0	$R - c$, $R - c$

One could question this result on the grounds that it covertly assumes away *commitment problems*. A commitment problem, according to Robert Frank, "arises when it is in a person's interest to make a binding commitment to behave in a way that will later seem contrary to self-interest" (1988, p. 47). An organizer may well claim that she will provide the good only if everyone contributes, but why should the organizer's resolve be taken seriously? If she secures enough funding to run the project at a profit, she will want to proceed with it whether or not she secures unanimity. Thus, it appears that the lone holdout can safely ignore her claim that she will not proceed without unanimity. This appearance, however, is no more than that, because willpower or stubbornness are not the factors on which the organizer's commitment depends. On the contrary, she cannot collect or spend *anyone's* contribution until she fulfills her end of the contract, and her end of the contract involves securing unanimous participation. If unanimous participation is one of the terms under which each participant is bound, then the lone holdout's refusal to contribute entails that the organizer will be not be able to collect or legally spend anyone else's contributions either. Thus, the structure of the contract itself ensures that prospective holdouts will be unable to turn the organizer's weakness of will to their advantage.

The assurance contract solves the assurance problem. In Case 3, we have also solved the free rider problem by building into the assurance contract a clause requiring unanimous participation. We have therefore solved the Prisoner's Dilemma. The assumption that everyone prefers R - c to zero (together with the assumption that everyone prefers zero to r - c, of course) defines the Prisoner's Dilemma. At the same time, this assumption is what gives the unanimity requirement its bite. Given this assumption, an assurance contract requiring unanimity makes contribution a dominant strategy for everyone.

Summary

Voluntary methods of producing public goods are subject to free rider and assurance problems. The assurance contract solves the assurance problem. Thus, for collective goods provided by means that exclude free riders, contribution becomes a dominant strategy for those who value R - c in excess of zero. Once the assurance problem is solved, contribution also becomes a dominant strategy when fringe benefits associated with providing the good are decisively large. In these cases, the assurance problem is solved and the free rider problem does not arise. When those involved all prefer mutual contribution to mutual withholding, as they do by hypothesis in the Prisoner's Dilemma, an assurance contract requiring unanimity can solve both free rider and assurance problems, provided only that an effective contractual enforcement mechanism is in place.

Seeking this solution has been worthwhile, if for no other reason than that many theorists would equate failing to discuss the Prisoner's Dilemma with ignoring the essence of the public goods problem. Unfortunately, while assurance contracts requiring unanimity may resolve Prisoner's Dilemmas, this entails neither that such contracts are emergently justified nor that they are teleologically justified as solutions to real-world public goods problems. The next chapter considers the moral and strategic implications of the fact that public goods problems are more complicated than the Prisoner's Dilemma model suggests.

5

From Prisoner's Dilemma to Public Goods

Complications

The previous chapter proposed a contractual resolution of the Prisoner's Dilemma. According to Barry and Hardin (1982, p. 109), the Prisoner's Dilemma is the most intractable form of the conflict between individual and collective interest. Be this as it may, the Prisoner's Dilemma is not the most intractable form of the public goods problem, for conflict between individual and collective interest is, unfortunately, only one facet of the public goods problem.

This chapter discusses additional complications created for public goods production when the assumptions that define the Prisoner's Dilemma are not quite true; also considered is the moral significance of these added complications. I discuss how contractual mechanisms not designed to solve Prisoner's Dilemmas might fare as solutions to public goods problems. Finding such mechanisms promising but flawed, I consider how they can be expected to function in comparison with more coercive alternatives. I also respond to an argument that contractual solutions, because they depend on essentially coercive contract enforcement mechanisms, are merely an alternative *kind* of coercion rather than an alternative *to* it, and thus are not emergently justified.

We said in Chapter 1 that the justification for coercive public goods provision arguably turns on a particularly benign kind of paternalism. Rolf Sartorius ably summarizes this view:

> The strong guiding hand of government will typically be required to lead individuals to make decisions whose collective effects will be mutually advantageous rather than mutually detrimental. The power to tax is, in this view, the power to compel individuals to contribute to the purchase of public goods that they would not be motivated to purchase for themselves. The power to make and enforce laws backed by coercive sanctions is, in this view, the power to provide individuals with reasons to act in ways that satisfy the general schema "If everyone (or a sufficiently large number of people) acted that way, everyone would be better off." (Sartorius, 1980, pp. 104-105)

According to this argument, the state is coercing people for their own good—and they know it. Moreover, they want the state to do this, because they cannot get what they want with voluntary provision mechanisms. Thus, one of the most attractive features of the public goods argument is the minimal nature of the normative assumptions it must make in order to ground a justification of the state. The public goods argument seems to presume only the legitimacy of helping people to do what they want to do but cannot do without the state's help. Yet this picture of the normative side of the coin, so readily accepted by political theorists, turns on an assumption that coercive public goods provision really does make us all better off.

But as Chapter 4 showed, the fact that a Prisoner's Dilemma incentive structure is present in a public goods problem is not itself a warrant for thinking force is necessary (over and beyond the amount and kind of force emergently justified by the fact that contractors have consented to its imposition).[1] I reached this conclusion by taking advantage of the strategic implications of the assumption embedded in the Prisoner's Dilemma: Everyone prefers mutual cooperation to mutual defection. Note that, given Chapter 4's assumption that preferences track interests, this is precisely the assumption embedded in Sartorius's schema "If everyone (or a sufficiently large number of people) acted that way, everyone would be better off." If we abandon the idea that the Prisoner's

Dilemma structure per se is the root of the public goods problem, we must allow that public goods problems may have a different kind of incentive structure such that public goods production requires coercion after all. (That is, it requires amounts and kinds of force that have not been emergently justified.) Once we open ourselves to this possibility, however, we also open ourselves to this question: If coercion is not solving Prisoner's Dilemmas, then what exactly is it doing for us? Until we answer this question, we cannot be sure that coercion is teleologically justified either.

The unanimity requirement discussed in Chapter 4 will usually be impractical, of course, but we cannot simply dismiss it on that ground. We must ask *why* it is impractical. Escaping the Prisoner's Dilemma presented itself as an end that could justify coercive means. But if the Prisoner's Dilemma is not really the problem we are solving, we cannot assume the practical end still packs the same normative punch. For example, in the AIDS research problem we might suppose the point of coercion is not to avoid free rider and assurance problems so much as to avoid the transaction costs of coming to voluntary agreements. But if a universally preferred cooperative solution is not what coercion produces, then what exactly is the objective that rationalizes coercive avoidance of transaction costs?

The actual interests different people have in particular public goods can vary widely; that a good exhibits characteristics of nonexclusiveness and nonrivalry in consumption does not guarantee that a given person has an interest in it. For any particular public good, there will be some people for whom it is not a good at all or, at least, has a total return too small to rationalize contributing c. Thus, for any particular project, those for whom the public good is of little or no value would thwart efforts to raise revenue via assurance contracts requiring unanimity. Such people would withhold not because of free rider or assurance problems (the assurance contract requiring unanimity has solved those) but simply because they *prefer* mutual withholding to mutual contribution.

A primary reason why requiring unanimity is impractical, then, is that there will almost always be people who refuse to participate simply because they do not attach significant value to the good in question. (We will call them *honest holdouts*.) The Prisoner's Dilemma model assumes such people away. (And even in cases where there are no honest holdouts, we will not know that fact. Hence, neither the practical nor the moral side of the problem allows us to assume them away.) But what are we to do? If we do not require honest holdouts to contribute, free riders will seek and probably find ways of passing themselves off as honest holdouts, and the whole fundraising scheme may disintegrate. Thus, the real point of coercion is to force even honest holdouts to pay and in that way assure that would-be free riders will not escape the fundraising scheme's contractual net.

Consequently, the kind of paternalistic argument I gave earlier for the coercive provision of public goods is not good enough. The prospect of justifying institutionalized coercion as a solution to public goods problems depends upon whether there is a prior justification for engaging in actions that can be expected to force some people (perhaps a minority, but not necessarily so) to help pay for other people's projects. Without this prior justification, the argument begs a most important question: Coercion may be necessary to force honest holdouts to help pay for other people's projects, but what exactly is it that makes pursuing this goal permissible in the first place? Merely pointing out that coercing these people is the most efficient way for others to get what they want does not even begin to discharge the burden of proof.

The major conclusion of this section, then—and one of the main conclusions of this book—is that the public goods argument is unsound. Its descriptive premise is that coercive public goods production makes each person better off from the person's own perspective. The argument's normative premise is that when coercion does this, coercion is permissible. The descriptive premise is, by and large, false. The normative premise is controversial but perhaps as unobjectionable as a normative premise could be and still retain sufficient substance to help teleologically justify coercive government. Without the descriptive premise, however, the permissibility of coercion does not follow from the normative premise. It takes a stronger, more controversial normative premise to derive the permissibility of coercion from the descriptive facts as they really are.

(Chapter 7 develops what I think is a more adequate normative basis for the public goods argument.)

Salvaging Unanimity

Can we repair the public goods argument without adding stronger and more controversial normative premises? We could, if we had some way to recognize honest holdouts and exclude them in advance from the group of which unanimity is required. The situation for those remaining would then be a Prisoner's Dilemma, and we know how to solve those. Ideally, an entrepreneur would devise a means of differentiating between people who do not want the good (given its price) and people who do and would then require contributions from members of the latter group only. Contribution would then be a dominant strategy for anyone who truly wants the good. (Technically, those who did not want the good would get a free ride, but the ride would not be worth much to them.) This solution would have practical as well as normative implications concerning fundraising for public goods production. In particular, it would weaken the case for coercion all the more. But such a solution is typically unavailable.

When there is no means of identifying honest holdouts in advance, some might think we can assume the existence of honest holdouts away on the ground that even though particular public goods are not universally desired, everyone nevertheless values the public goods production system as a whole. If so, the mutual advantageousness of the system as a whole can be the basis of its benign paternalistic justification. (But even if we know *some* system is justifiable in this way, we still have the problem of making sure that the system we actually pick is justifiable in this way.) For a system that can be so justified, the overarching public goods problem of producing such a system would be a Prisoner's Dilemma. If we were able to identify such a system, and if the Prisoner's Dilemma structure itself was really the impediment to its success, a voluntary contract (similar in scope to what political theorists call a social contract) would present itself as a possibility.

Of course, if we were talking about, say, 100,000 people, the contract would not require unanimity. Requiring unanimity on that scale would, I suppose, be foolish. It would be almost as foolish, however, to assume that they would each prefer mutual cooperation (especially mutual cooperation achieved by force) to mutual defection. Thus, unanimity becomes an increasingly unrealistic solution to *n*-person Prisoner's Dilemmas as *n* rises, but it is also true that it becomes increasingly unrealistic to suppose that the situation is a Prisoner's Dilemma at all as *n* rises. Thus, switching our focus from individual public goods to public goods producing systems does not change the fact that the paternalistic justification for coercive provision becomes increasingly implausible at the same time as unanimity becomes an increasingly implausible route to voluntary provision.

In practice, of course, voluntary contracts often would not require unanimity. They would have to attract members with judicious mixes of collective goods that included exclusive and otherwise unavailable goods (as per Olson, pp. 132ff). Moreover, if we were to try to secure a social contract, i.e., a contractual agreement to a system devised to produce a variety of public goods, we would have an additional problem. As with package deals in general, people might find themselves forced to decide for or against packages that included items few people have any use for. Efficiency would be increased by distributing the funds raised by the package-deal contract in accordance with relative group demand for each good within the package. This could be done by giving each contributor the option of distributing at least part of her total contribution as she wishes among the separate projects in the package (subject, perhaps, to a restriction that every good in the package receive a specified minimum level of funding). A contributor who exercised this option would then have an additional assurance that most of her money, at least, would be spent only on projects she found most worthwhile. (Note that the proceeds of coercive fundraising mechanisms also could be distributed, in whole or in part, in this manner.)

Let us review the territory we have covered: (1) If we know there are no honest holdouts, we do not need coercion. We can simply require unanimity as a precondition of the contract's validity. (2) If there are honest holdouts but we can tell them apart from others, we do not need coercion. We can require unanimity among those who are not honest holdouts. (3) If we believe there are honest holdouts but cannot identify them, then we may need coercion, but in that case justifying coercion requires us to justify using some as means to the ends of others.

Thus, if we believe that an appropriate contractual offer (a binding and final choice between mutual withholding and mutual cooperation) requiring unanimity could be made but we still believe that coercion would be necessary, we must believe either that some people would rationally prefer mutual withholding to mutual cooperation under the circumstances or that some people would irrationally prefer mutual withholding. (In other words, the assumption of Chapter 4 that preferences track interests would be false in their cases.) What is really driving us to give up voluntary unanimous solutions is our belief that not everyone is rational and that among those people who are, not all of them want what we want them to pay for. Hence, the assumption of the legitimacy of benign paternalism must be augmented by more controversial assumptions regarding the legitimacy both of stronger forms of paternalism and of forcing some people to pay for other people's projects.

Admittedly, honest holdouts and irrational holdouts are not the only kinds of noncontributors with which a society must contend. Many perfectly rational people might fail to contribute because of ignorance, avoidable or otherwise. Be this as it may, the point is not that people who think coercion is necessary have no alternative to believing either that there are honest holdouts or that some people are irrational. The point, rather, is that there really are honest holdouts and there really are irrational people, and the premise that coercion helps people satisfy their desires is, in these cases, false. Hence, the legitimacy of helping such people satisfy their desires cannot get us to the legitimacy of forcing them to help produce public goods that they do not in fact want.

If we want everyone to contribute and are willing to use coercion to assure it, we have difficult moral territory to cover. The justification we must seek is teleological. To wit, if we trust others to make up their own minds, some of them will ruin things for the rest of us out of ignorance or spite or because they honestly do not want what the rest of us want. In Chapter 6, I present experimental evidence that people do not always contribute to public goods projects even when circumstances have been contrived to render contribution a dominant strategy with respect to the monetary interests at stake. These data are particularly telling evidence that public goods problems are not solely—perhaps not even mainly—conflicts between individual and collective interest.

Unanimity in the sense of requiring each member of a set of individuals to contribute is not practical on a large scale, barring a means of identifying in advance those who would choose mutual withholding over mutual contribution. It might be considerably more practical, however, to require unanimous contribution from neighborhood associations, for example, rather than to require unanimous contribution from each individual member of those groups. The representatives of several neighborhood associations, for example, might unanimously agree to help build a central recreational facility and then leave each other to solve the problem of mustering support within their individual associations. Corporations also seem to operate on roughly this principle when they offer matching grants to charitable foundations. A corporation will not require contribution from every member of a foundation, but it will require an appropriate contribution from the foundation as a whole. How the foundation induces its membership to produce its share is left up to the foundation. Thus, matching grants are examples of assurance contracts that (often successfully) require unanimous contribution not by individuals but by representatives of larger groups.

Asymmetrical Payoffs

The next section will say more about assurance contracts that do not require unanimity. In this section, we consider problems that can arise when attempting to produce public goods by coercion. As I said in Chapter 1, part of the point of studying voluntary solutions to public goods problems is that coercive solutions are very often unavailable. At other times, coercive fundraising is possible but the prevalence of honest holdouts renders doubtful its desirability. The use of force is, at least theoretically, a simple solution to the problems with voluntary mechanisms. This simplicity is in some respects more apparent than real, however, for coercion quickly becomes complicated indeed when we turn to the question of how to control the controllers. The central insight of what is known as the *public choice* school of economics is that a person does not cease to be interested in personal gain merely by virtue of acquiring the powers of a Leviathan. In fact, once the Leviathan secures his power, there may be little to stop him from exploiting it to the fullest. (The classic source on this subject is Buchanan and Tullock, 1962.) Although the historically first and normatively primary function of government is to protect its citizens from negative externalities, including those its citizens would impose on each other, it remains the case that government is itself an imposer of negative externalities without rival. The social cost of its activities is largely borne not by it but by taxpayers. Current government spending patterns strongly suggest that the tragedy of the commons in land, averted by the institution (or evolution) of entitlements, has reemerged as a tragedy of the commons in income—those with access to political power and hence to tax revenues are able to finance their projects without regard to whether the income they are spending is their own. In line with the logic of the commons, they show no inclination to exercise restraint (although they exhort each other to do so).

Thus, the public choice literature has taught us that, although people may not take the external effects of their actions into account, this cuts both ways when it comes to forcing them to contribute to public goods projects. On the one hand, voluntary solutions to the public goods problem will typically be inefficient because people will withhold even in some cases where cooperation has a higher collective payoff. They will not take the social benefits of their contributions fully into account. Coercive solutions, on the other hand, can ensure cooperation but will typically be inefficient because government officials often enforce cooperation even when withholding has a higher collective payoff. They do not take the social cost of spending other people's money fully into account.

Hence, for the same reason that markets are inherently underactive in the production of public goods, governments are inherently overactive. They inherently tend to expand to levels in excess of what would be efficient (in the sense of equating marginal social cost to marginal social benefit). If the building of dams is funded by voluntary mechanisms, then we would expect a suboptimal number of dams. If dam-building is funded by taxation, then we would expect some dams to be built simply because a few people with access to political power benefit a great deal from such projects. As special interest groups acquire the power to set the agenda for coercive public goods production, the class of honest holdouts who are forced to contribute can swell to the point of becoming a vast majority. Whether coercive over-production is more efficient than market under-production in a given case will be an empirical matter, but at least there is a limit to how costly under-production can be, for the worst that can happen is that the good is not produced at all.

Figure 5.1
Special Interest Groups and the Risk of Overproduction

		Player/Subgroup 2 contributes?	
		NO	YES
Player/Subgroup 1 contributes?	NO	0 0	less than 1 0
	YES	0 -3	1 -2

Figure 5.1 formalizes the depiction of special interest group politics, where asymmetrical payoffs allow a special interest minority to profit by using coercion to exploit the majority, which has become an entire class of honest holdouts. In Figure 5.1, the uncoerced outcome evidently would be optimal. (The optimal outcome is the upper left or the upper right box, depending on whether "less than 1" is more than zero. We would expect player 1 to withhold in any event and player 2 to then be willing and able to produce the optimal outcome, whichever it is.)[2] However, the matrix also depicts a common occurrence—an asymmetric distribution of cooperative benefits. This imbalance leads subgroups of the collective to invest energy struggling for access to the government's coercive power. Things become even worse if the struggle should happen to be won by subgroup 2. In that event, although cooperation may cost more than it is worth (the sum of benefits will be negative unless subgroup 1 is relatively small), cooperation will be the end result. The collective's loss purchases the subgroup's gain.

The asymmetries of benefits that compromise the effectiveness of coercive mechanisms can be turned to the advantage of voluntary mechanisms. The more concentrated the benefits are, the better the assurance contract will work, because asymmetry will boost the marginal rate of return for some subgroup relative to a given marginal gain for the group as a whole. In Figure 5.1, the average payoff of mutual cooperation for players 1 and 2 is -0.5, so if both players were actually average in this respect, there would be no opportunity to cooperate for mutual gain. On the other hand, the players of subgroup 2 may have an opportunity for mutually profitable cooperation among themselves, because although the average payoff is negative, the cooperative payoff for players in subgroup 2 is actually +1. (The situation in which only subgroup 2 contributes is reflected in the upper right box of Figure 5.1. I show the payoff for subgroup 2 in this situation as being less than 1, leaving open the possibility that the payoff of cooperation solely among members of subgroup 2 might, after all, be greater than zero.)

Assurance Contracts Without Unanimity

The previous discussion has a bearing on the prospect of solving public goods problems with assurance contracts. Figure 5.2 depicts the payoffs for Jane when an assurance contract requires unanimity. (The payoffs for the rest of the group are not shown.) In situation X, the assurance contract will fail regardless of Jane's strategy (i.e., someone else will withhold). In situation Y, Jane's contribution is just sufficient for the assurance contract to succeed (i.e., the rest of the group are going to contribute). If these are the only two possible situations, then contributing c is obviously a dominant strategy for those who value R in excess of c.

Figure 5.2
Payoffs of Assurance Contract Requiring Unanimity

Enough Others Contribute to Satisfy the Contract?

		X	Y
Jane contributes?	NO	0	0
	YES	0	$R - c$

(X = not enough, Y = just enough if Jane contributes)

To make the discussion somewhat more concrete, let us suppose that the case at hand involves an assurance contract telethon to raise money for AIDS research. Jane is wondering whether to pick up the telephone and make a pledge. If we drop the unanimity requirement altogether, as public goods problems typically would force us to do, the assurance contract will require no particular percentage of people to participate but only that the total amount pledged reaches a certain target. (Let the target be n

contributions of c and let the total return from an investment meeting the target be R.) Thus, the assurance contract can succeed even if some players do prefer mutual withholding to mutual cooperation. Dropping the unanimity requirement, however, makes possible a third situation, where the assurance contract succeeds regardless of whether Jane makes a pledge (although project output is less by r than it would have been had Jane contributed). This is depicted as situation Z in Figure 5.3.

Figure 5.3
Payoffs of Assurance Contract Not Requiring Unanimity

Enough Others Contribute to Satisfy the Contract?

Jane contributes?	X	Y	Z
NO	0	0	$R - r$
YES	0	$R - c$	$R - c$

(X = not enough, Y = just enough if Jane contributes, Z = at least enough even if Jane does not contribute)

Situation X is as it was in Figure 5.2; the contract will not secure enough funds to be valid even if Jane does pledge c. Situation Y is also as it was in Figure 5.2; Jane's pledge is just sufficient to make the contract succeed. Jane's pledge may not be necessary, though. Because unanimity is not required, it is only clearly necessary that someone pledges to contribute.

In situation Z, a sufficient contribution has already been made. In situation Z, there would generally be contributions in excess of what was required by the assurance contract. This excess could be returned either as a rebate, a lottery prize, or as increased production levels. (Of course, increased production levels would imply that the R in situation Z is larger than the R in situation Y.)

Although situation X is the worst possible outcome for those who value *R* in excess of *c*, many players may hold out in the hope of finding themselves in situation Z, where they may enjoy a free ride. Cooperation will not be a dominant strategy as long as players can hope to receive *R* without contributing *c*. On the other hand, note that withholding is not a dominant strategy either. Because of the assurance contract, as we can see in Figure 5.3, withholding does not become a dominant strategy even when the unanimity requirement cannot be used to eliminate situation Z. In Figure 5.3, there is no dominant strategy. The lower middle box, however, where Jane makes a pledge and thereby ensures the contract's success, depicts a Nash equilibrium; that is, contributors in that situation would have an incentive not to change their strategy unilaterally. Of course, contributors would be contractually bound not to change their strategy in any event.

Would mutual withholding also be a Nash equilibrium? Let us separate this into two questions. First, do withholders have an incentive not to change their strategy inilaterally? No. On the contrary, unilaterally changing to a YES strategy would be free, except for transaction costs (the cost of a phone call in a telethon, which would presumably have a toll-free number) and opportunity costs associated with leaving committed resources in liquid form (presumably negligible in a telethon time frame). Thus, a Nash equilibrium in the strong sense that players have a positive reason not to unilaterally depart from it is not present here. Mutual withholding, however, is a Nash equilibrium in a weaker sense—although there may be no reason not to change strategy unilaterally, nor is there obvious reason *to* change unilaterally. Jane does no better unilaterally contributing than by withholding. But since Jane does no worse either, given the assurance contract guarantee, withholding is an equilibrium in a very weak sense indeed. In fact, by this standard, unilateral contribution is also an equilibrium. Neither equilibrium is at all stable. Whether a situation of mutual withholding ultimately collapses (as players unilaterally decide that they might as well cooperate) will depend upon factors not captured by the matrix. (Note that the corresponding collapse of situation Z is precluded by the contract. Once committed, players cannot change their minds.)

What factors might lead players to contribute? On the one hand, if Jane believes herself to be in situation Y (see Figure 5.3), she has an incentive to contribute. Contribution is a Nash equilibrium strategy in the strong sense in situation Y: Those who have already made pledges no longer have the option of changing their strategy, and if those who have not made pledges continue to hold out, an individual in situation Y is better off pledging to contribute c. On the other hand, suppose Jane believes that, as the deadline approaches, so many other people will jump on the bandwagon that her chances of being able to free ride are very good. If the target is reached before the deadline, then those who have not yet contributed will make their decisions knowing that they are in situation Z and that their contribution is not necessary. In this case, the assurance contract has succeeded and the (AIDS research) public goods problem has been solved without their help. If the target is not reached before the deadline, then as the deadline approaches, an uncommitted Jane's evaluation of her chances of having a free ride must become more pessimistic as she waits for a surge of pledges that fails to materialize. At the final moment, Jane must balance her dwindling chance of ending up in situation Z against her dwindling chance of ending up in situation Y.

However this balancing is resolved, its result may be less important than the incentives stemming from the increasing chance that uncommitted players will end up in situation X. Suppose that as the deadline approaches, an as yet uncommitted Jane comes to believe, with increasing justification, that she is in situation X. If so, then she has a positive (albeit weak) reason to switch unilaterally to a YES strategy. First, the matrix in Figure 5.3 makes it appear as if she has nothing to lose by holding out in situation X, but in a sense this is not true. Holdout behavior (i.e., failing to switch from NO to YES) is costly. With the assurance contract, if those who have yet to make a pledge hold out too long, the conditionally binding commitments already obtained from other players will be forfeited, because such commitments are subject to the contract deadline. These previously made commitments are valuable, and Jane will lose them if the situation does not change.

Consider how a person averse to risk might view this situation.

Without an assurance contract, the assurance problem will tend to deter a risk-averse person more than it would a risk-neutral maximizer of expected utility. At the same time, a risk-averse person would have as much inclination as anyone else to free ride; the essential characteristic of a free rider is not that he maximizes expected personal utility, but that he avoids paying his share of the cost of collective goods. For example, a *maximin strategy* (playing so as to avoid the worst case scenario) is perfectly consistent with the inclination to free ride, because the worst case scenario is the one in which the individual contributes but no one else does. Withholding, even if it does not result in a free ride, at least avoids the worst case.

That withholding avoids the worst case, however, holds true only as long as the assurance problem remains unsolved. The same risk-aversion that would normally lead a person to withhold on to the chance that his contribution would be wasted, actually works to the advantage of a project employing the assurance contract because in this situation the worst case consists of the good not being provided. And pledging to contribute minimizes the probability of the worst case. (The cost of making a pledge might also make the worst case marginally worse, but one can be risk-averse without quibbling over incidentals.) Thus, with an assurance contract, those who play maximin strategies will contribute as the deadline approaches, if not before.

Another function the approaching deadline might serve is to make Jane more conscious of a sense of moral obligation to do her share—if the fundraiser fails, it will be partly her fault. The approaching deadline begins to make her inaction look increasingly culpable. If there is a money-back guarantee to ensure that contributing will not be a foolish waste, this sense of moral responsibility may make a big difference to her in the moments immediately before the deadline.[3]

Unfortunately, if Jane is in situation X, then by assumption she cannot by herself make the difference between failure and success of the contract. She could do this only if she were in situation Y. Nevertheless, although Jane cannot herself make the crucial pledge, her pledge might put as yet uncommitted players in situation Y. If

Jane makes a pledge, the worst that can happen is that it will not be collected. There is reason not to contribute; yet, at the same time, when all things are considered, at least she cannot lose by contributing. (She can get less than she would have gotten by free riding, of course, but $R - c$ is still a gain.) To be precise, the worst she can do is end up not being compensated for the opportunity cost of holding her pledge liquid while waiting to see if the contract succeeds. Whether the considerations discussed here can induce people to pass up the chance of getting a free ride is an empirical matter to be pursued in Chapter 6.

Market Anarchy

The efficacy of the money-back guarantee assumes the existence of a reliable vehicle for enforcing the terms of that guarantee. Thus, assurance contracts would be no help to a group whose goal was to establish a mechanism for enforcing contracts in the first place. We need to discuss this not because it matters how things arise from the state of nature but because the problem has implications for the moral status of contract enforcement here and now.

I have taken assurance contracts to be emergently justified on the grounds that they arise by consent. But whether this is so might be thought to depend on whether the *enforcement mechanism* upon which they essentially depend is emergently justified. Michael Taylor claims that "the maintenance of a system of sanctions itself constitutes or presupposes the solution of another collective action problem" (1987, p. 30). We might put the argument as follows: The state must use coercion both as a means of raising funds for contract enforcement and also as the instrument of contract enforcement. Both kinds of coercion are essential to the working of assurance contracts. Thus, assurance contracts (and anything else that relies on contract enforcement) are merely coercion in a different form rather than a genuine alternative to it.

My response to this argument is two-fold. First, coercion is not necessary to finance contract enforcement. Note that contract enforcement is not a public good. There is rivalry in consumption; providing the service to additional consumers is costly. Although there is presumably a more or less fixed cost of developing the basic capability of enforcing contracts, there is also a per-unit cost involved in undertaking the protection of each discrete contract. The benefit of paying for enforcement of a particular contract would extend only to that particular contract. Nor is contract enforcement nonexclusive; it can be sold by competitive firms to parties willing to pay for it either in advance or by such means as they stipulate among the other conditions of their contracts.

People would not be able to free ride on the general deterrent effect of other people's contributions for contract enforcement because the deterrent effect would be relevant only to those who have paid to become subject to it. If Jane's contract makes no arrangements for its own enforcement, the upshot is not that the general *level* of enforcement suffers a slight drop but rather that the *scope* of enforcement is not extended to protect Jane; Jane's contract is not enforced.

So contract enforcement can be provided noncoercively by the private sector, so long as the benefit of enforcing a contract is sufficient to cover the cost and so long as the state does not crowd out the private sector by offering an acceptable tax-funded substitute. Bouckaert (unpublished) details how some goods such as contract enforcement came to be viewed in Europe as public goods only after their provision was undertaken by governments, with the consequence that providing similar services by charging user fees was no longer feasible.[4] Nor is private sector provision of contract arbitration (albeit within a framework of public contract enforcement) unknown today, despite government provision of a competitive product free of charge to users. (See Koenig, 1984 and Sitomer, 1988.)

The other issue raised in this section concerned the legitimacy of using force as the instrument of contract enforcement. This legitimacy derives from the consent of the involved parties. An agency that enforces compliance by the principals is doing only what the principals have hired it to do. One of the clauses of the contract everyone signs stipulates that if anyone reneges, an enforcer is permitted to collect the delinquent payment plus, perhaps, a penalty that the enforcer can keep as a fee for service. The paradigmatically emergent justification for this use of force is based on actual consent. Anyone subject to it has literally asked for it. In writing.

Premarket Anarchy and the Concatenated Prisoner's Dilemma

This does not quite settle the issue of whether assurance contracts presume coercive background institutions. We may be able to push the argument of the preceding section one step back. Any market's emergence presupposes a means of enforcing the terms of agreements regarding commodities to be exchanged. True, if contract enforcement were sold as a private good, people would pay for it—if they had some assurance of getting what they paid for. But what could provide such assurance in the first place, when contract enforcement agencies have not yet established themselves? It appears that, because prior agreements to enforce contracts are themselves contractual relationships, markets for the commodity of contract enforcement presuppose their own existence. Arguably, they cannot arise by a market process because their existence is required *before* market processes themselves can arise. Jules Coleman (1985) calls this *premarket market failure*.

Let us see where we stand. The previous section defended assurance contracts against the charge that the enforcement institution they presuppose is coercive. Now we must consider whether contract enforcement, although not coercive in its operation, nevertheless presupposes some other coercive process for its emergence. If the emergence of contract enforcement mechanisms depends on coercion, then those mechanisms are not emergently justified—and (we might argue) neither is anything that depends on them.

Yet suppose that the emergence of contract enforcement mechanisms was coercive as a matter of fact, but only contingently so. In other words, suppose that the enforcement institution on which the assurance contract depends happened to come about by coercion, but noncoercive processes could have produced similar institutions had they not been preempted by coercive ones. In this case, although assurance contracts rely on the operation of a mechanism for enforcing contracts, they do not rely on the coercive process by which operative contract enforcement happens to have emerged. In other words, if enforcement mechanisms can emerge without coercion, then when an assurance contract counts on enforcement mechanisms, it does not count on those mechanisms emerging by coercion. (And the assurance contracts themselves, of course, emerge by voluntary consent.) Thus, the emergent justification of the assurance contract depends on finding that its enforcement mechanism operates noncoercively *in fact* and that the history of such mechanisms is noncoercive in *principle*. (For the enforcement mechanism itself to be emergently justified, its history would have to be noncoercive in fact as well as in principle. But the assurance contract's emergent justification turns on its own history, not on the history of the enforcement mechanisms it relies on. It is necessary only that in counting on an enforcement mechanism being in place, it is not at the same time counting on that mechanism emerging by coercion.)

So, can we show that contract enforcement mechanisms can, in principle, emerge without coercion? I believe that a market could bootstrap itself out of the chaos of premarket market failure via the potential for people to develop reputations as reliable trading partners. I admit that if a society is too large or too impersonal to permit the development of reputations, premarket market failure may have no solution. But then, that very supposition suggests that the community would not remain so large and impersonal. The scope of people's interactions initially would contract to a point where people dealt only with people they could trust, perhaps in the end only with familiar faces. People would develop a strong preference for dealing with people with whom they have had previous experience and with whom they expected to have subsequent dealings. Hence, one way or another, market forces would resolve premarket market failure.

The scope of commercial activity would be determined by the efficacy of such technology as existed for transmitting information of the kind that constitutes a reputation (i.e, word of mouth, at first). In turn, the scope of activity thus determined would expand as technological advance created circumstances in which people could safely deal with relative strangers. In sum, it is surely true that market forces suffice to drive the emergence of markets in general. Witness the emergence and gradual expansion of markets even in countries where very powerful governments are committed to stamping them out.

Could market forces also drive the emergence of markets for contract enforcement in particular? This is a more difficult question. If the premarket situation permits the development of reputations, as it well might, then an agency whose actions identified it as a reliable private supplier would simultaneously create and capture the emerging market for contract enforcement. In this situation, only buyers and sellers who cooperate will do repeat business and only they will get the kind of reputation that attracts new business. The situation is not a Prisoner's Dilemma nor even an *iterated* Prisoner's Dilemma. (The latter is a game in which a player faces a sequence of ordinary "one-shot" Prisoner's Dilemmas with the same opponent.) It is what I call a *concatenated* Prisoner's Dilemma, meaning that as one iterated Prisoner's Dilemma game comes to an end, the buyer and seller enter into other iterated Prisoner's Dilemmas with different partners. To the extent that players know each other's history, reliable trading partners gravitate toward each other. Thus, part of the payoff to Jane in a concatenated game is that the reliability of her future partners is not a random variable; instead, it is a function of her own reliability. This extra payoff makes the concatenated game different from the ordinary iterated game.

Each discrete game can be viewed in isolation as an iterated Prisoner's Dilemma, but viewing the games in isolation is a mistake. Jane's defection in one game not only precludes repeat business with that partner in that game; rather, by affecting the reputation she brings to other games, it also limits the payoffs she can realize in her other games. To the extent that reputation travels from one game to the next, the brunt of the negative externalities she creates by defecting in one game will fall squarely on her as a player of other games. If there are players who value ongoing relationships with reliable partners more than the free rider payoff of any single game, and if these players can find each other, the market for contract enforcement will emerge.

It is commonly held that in a finitely iterated Prisoner's Dilemma where players know when the game will end, players will automatically defect in the last period, because there is no ongoing relationship to worry about. And because they will automatically defect in the final period, they may as well defect in the next to last period too. The logic zips backward, implying that the only rational strategy is to defect right from the start.[5] But none of this follows if (in a game between you and Jane) Jane comes to the game with an established reputation for always responding to her partner's moves in kind. If you think Jane will live up to her reputation, then the rational strategy for you is not to defect from the start but rather to cooperate until the game is nearly over, in order to elicit the maximally cooperative response from Jane. (This idea comes from Kreps, et al., 1982.) This holds even in the ordinary iterated game, as long as players can have previously established reputations going into the game.

Moreover, if the situation is a concatenated Prisoner's Dilemma rather than merely an iterated one, then reputation can operate not only within games but between them as well. In this case, the way for Jane to preserve her reputation for playing tit-for-tat is to cooperate even in the final period of her game with you, unless you defect first. Although you may free ride on her in the final period, it will be her, not you, who acquires a reputation for being a desirable partner. She ends up being able to select other final-period cooperators as her partners; you, in contrast, have to settle for partners who reason that since you have a reputation for defecting in the last period, they might as well defect in the second last period, and so on.[6]

This is not to deny that there is still an assurance problem in the premarket situation, but the profits associated with establishing a reputation for reliability make mutual cooperation more profitable than free riding in the long run. Hence, buyers and sellers who have an interest in the long run need only find each other. For them, the concatenated Prisoner's Dilemma lets buyers know which sellers deliver as promised, thus opening the door to an immensely lucrative market for the private good of contract enforcement. And the first to cooperate stands to be first through the door.

Private sector provision of contract enforcement, it should be noted, is more than just a hypothetical case. The *Law Merchant*, for example, arose spontaneously in medieval Europe in response to the needs of international merchants for a body of law that transcended political boundaries. (See Trakman, 1983.) Hence we have ample reason to think legitimate mechanisms for contract arbitration and enforcement can emerge—indeed they *have* emerged—via market forces.

The warning in the previous section should perhaps be repeated here. My speculations are not motivated by an interest in the state of nature but rather by a concern about the nature of the background institutions presupposed by assurance contracts. Because contract enforcement is not coercive in its operation and is not essentially coercive in its emergence, such coercion as might contingently manifest itself in the actual history of contract enforcement's emergence is not what assurance contracts rely on and so does not taint them. Thus, employing assurance contracts in a society like ours would be emergently justified even if they depend on an enforcement mechanism that itself is not emergently justified—provided the contracts themselves emerge by consent.

On Choosing Between Markets and Government

Producing public goods has effects that spill over onto people not involved in the production process. This creates both free rider and assurance problems. But these problems are not sufficient to justify using coercion to raise funds for public goods provision, for they are not enough to make coercion necessary. When we also consider that there will be honest holdouts as well as free riders, we have a situation in which cooperation cannot be made a dominant strategy by contractual means. At the same time, if coercion is used, the point of using it will be to force honest holdouts to pay so that free riders have nothing to gain by impersonating them.

It is only in situations in which some people (who cannot be identified in advance) have no strong desire (or do not know that they do) for public goods even in general that the assurance contract must leave the free rider problem unresolved. Although the assurance contract might nevertheless succeed, leaving the free rider problem unsolved means that some public goods projects might not receive adequate funding even if the assurance contract was used. If emergently justified mechanisms, such as the assurance contract, were tried without success, then the next step would be to determine whether coercive alternatives are teleologically justified under the same circumstances. We cannot assume, when voluntary methods do not work well, that coercion will work better—or even that coercion will be a real option. Chapter 6 reviews experimental tests of voluntary methods of public goods financing that bear on the arguments of this chapter and Chapter 4. Chapter 7 considers the morality of forcing people to contribute.

In this chapter, I explored and rejected the possibility that the assurance contract is derivatively coercive because its efficacy depends on the existence of a coercive contract enforcement mechanism. It relies on some kind of contract enforcement mechanism, to be sure, but it does not rely on that mechanism being coercive. And we saw that this point applies not only to the mechanism's operation but to its origin as well. Thus the assurance contract is a genuine alternative to coercion.

We should view market solutions to public goods problems with the same kind of healthy skepticism as we would view a postcard. We know from experience that when we actually get there, things may not look as good as they did in the postcard. If the market was unable to adequately provide public goods, this might lead us to want our government to have more power than would make sense if the market was more efficacious. But this caution also needs qualifying. A more powerful government looks better in the postcard too. We would do well not to assume that the extra power we might invest in it will be used as we intend.

6

Experimental Philosophy

As discussed in Chapter 4, the problem of producing public goods by collective action takes the form of a Prisoner's Dilemma when the marginal return per unit of contribution is less than one unit to the contributor but more than one unit to the group. Thus, although the group is strictly better off if a given unit is contributed rather than withheld, the individuals in the group are strictly better off if they withhold their contributions. Because the members of the group decide as individuals rather than as a group, the assumption that individuals act so as to maximize personal wealth implies that individuals in a Prisoner's Dilemma situation will contribute exactly nothing.

I have defended assurance contracts on theoretical grounds as a device for eliciting contributions to public goods projects. But theory and practice, one might say, have a way of diverging. Accordingly, two questions cry out for discussion. First, how serious is the empirical public goods problem? Second, how effective is the assurance contract as an empirical solution to this empirical problem? To answer these questions, this chapter turns to the methods of experimental economics.

Field Data and Controlled Experiments

In 1979, the Association of Oregon Faculties wanted to raise $30,000 to hire a lobbyist to represent them at the state legislature.

They sought $36, $60, or $84 contributions, depending on salary, from all faculty in the state. The drive was successful (Dawes, et al., 1986, p. 1172). In 1980 and 1985, Canada's New Democratic Party attempted to raise $200,000 and $250,000 respectively in campaign contributions. They succeeded both times, with $1,300 to spare in the second case (Bagnoli and McKee, forthcoming, p. 1). In each case, funds were solicited on the understanding that they would be returned to donors if the target figure was not reached. These are examples of fundraising mechanisms with the structure of assurance contracts working well in the real world.

Yet it is not clear what we can safely infer from such examples. How well would the same fundraising drives have worked without the money-back guarantee? We can only guess whether this feature made a significant difference. Of course, our problem is hardly unusual. Field experiments are almost always uncontrolled in the technical sense. That is, we want to hold all variables constant, except for a single target variable, so that we may learn how the outcome is affected specifically by changes in the target variable. But in the field, holding all other variables constant is next to impossible, which means there will almost always be a variety of explanations for the experimental outcome. Hence, assessing the importance of changes in the target variable (the fundraising mechanism in this case) is typically very difficult. This is just one example of a traditional problem with the scientific approach to economics. When field data seem to disconfirm an applicable theory, it is often just as reasonable to reject the data as it is to reject the theory, because the data are gathered under conditions that do not permit proper control over the set of possibly relevant variables. Nor is control the only problem. Some relevant variables, such as the value people attach to the hiring of a state lobbyist, are not even observable, let alone controllable. In-principle testability has been a feature of most important theories in economics (i.e., they have empirical content). Practical testability has been another matter entirely.

Laboratory conditions, however, offer the possibility of greater control, particularly over such ordinarily unobservable variables as preferences, knowledge endowments, and strategies of the agents involved (Smith, unpublished). To determine how behavior is affected by institutions and environments, we need information about and control over these key variables, which are not controllable or even observable in the field. In the laboratory, inherently private valuations can be stipulated by and hence known to the experimenter. That is, we can specify the resale value to each subject of a given unit at the same time as we strip the unit of all properties other than price and resale value. Thus, while valuations are private information in the sense that subjects do not know what value a unit has to other subjects, the experimenter can, for example, see exactly how actual contribution levels compare with optimal contribution levels or how actual behavior compares with demand-revealing behavior. (I.e., do subjects offer as much as the unit is worth to them, or do they underbid?) We thereby learn much about the strategies subjects employ. And because the experimental instructions are generally the only source of information subjects have about the nature of the experiment, knowledge endowments are well controlled too. Thus, the usual response to field experiments—that when a theory is not corroborated, something is wrong with the experiment—is not so easily defended as a response to data gathered in the laboratory.

The Isaac-Walker Design

An extremely general (and hence very powerful) model of the public goods problem has been tested in the laboratory by Isaac, Walker, and Thomas (1984) and by Isaac and Walker (1988). In these experiments, subjects (4 or 10 in a group) were given an initial endowment of tokens and asked to allot them between private and public exchanges. A token invested in the *private exchange* yielded one cent to the individual subject. A token invested in the *public exchange* yielded a sum to be divided equally among all subjects in the group. (The size of the sum was determined by the group's production function. Two such functions were used, both linear, yielding either 0.3 or 0.75 cents per subject for each token invested in the public exchange.) A series of ten trials allowed subjects to learn that their single-period dominant strategy was to invest all of their income in the private exchange. Subjects were told in advance that the tenth period would be the final period so that their single-period dominant strategy would clearly be salient in the tenth period.

The results of these experiments disconfirmed the prediction that investment in the public exchange in period 10 will be zero. Even in end periods preceded by what should have been ample opportunity to learn dominant strategies, contributions are positive and substantial, albeit suboptimal. Why do subjects contribute as much as they do? Why do they contribute anything at all? Since our set of assumptions implies a prediction that contributions will be precisely zero in period 10, the fact that this prediction is consistently wrong suggests that one of our assumptions is false. Because noncontribution is clearly a dominant strategy, a process of elimination locates the error in our behavioral assumption that subjects act so as to maximize personal income.

Perhaps some subjects simply do not behave strategically. That is, they may develop some expectation of how much of the public good will be produced and then simply contribute what they are willing to pay for that product. Some subjects may operate by rules of thumb (like "Make small contributions to charity.") and thus may be oblivious to the incentives involved in particular situations. (Failure to grasp the nature of the incentives could also lead some subjects to contribute, although one might expect that subjects who did not understand the situation would be more likely to "sit tight" and contribute nothing. Moreover, the situation was by no means complicated; I think failure to comprehend does play a role in what we observe, but by the tenth period, only a very small one.) Or perhaps the preferences of others enter into the preference functions of subjects. That is, subjects prefer to benefit other subjects. Or perhaps some subjects, if they are wealth maximizers at all, place certain constraints upon what they will do to maximize personal wealth. In other words, the externalities involved in the decision to contribute or not may enter into subjects' decisions as part of their set of constraints, along with income constraints and so on. Subjects may not exactly have an interest in or preference for benefiting other subjects but may not consider it permissible to fail to do their share, whatever they perceive their share to be. Many of those who contribute even in final periods may be constrained rather than straightforward maximizers, to use David Gauthier's terms (1986, pp. 160ff).

Contributing positive but suboptimal amounts in experimental situations is sometimes described as "weak" free riding. This label may mask the likelihood that the phenomenon so named is not free riding at all. Some individuals may contribute suboptimally not because they are free riders, weak or otherwise, but because they are averse to being, so to speak, taken for a ride. Let us call the aversion to being taken advantage of an *exploitation* problem. Subjects with an exploitation problem seek some assurance that the pattern of contributions within the group will be fair before they will contribute what they believe to be their share.[1] Alternatively, when the interests of others are obviously at stake, and where a person obviously has interests in the decisions made by those others, a person may be willing to compromise and make positive contributions on the understanding that a mutually profitable degree of reciprocation will be forthcoming. A person's contributions, however, may be limited to a level such that the sum of investments in the public exchange can be expected to yield a return sufficient to repay his own investment. This limitation is an *assurance* problem.

If problems such as the assurance problem are among the reasons why people contribute positive but suboptimal amounts, then the assurance contract is promising whether or not it makes contributing a dominant strategy. On the one hand, the hypothesis that people will free ride whenever they have the opportunity is disconfirmed by experiments such as those conducted by Isaac and Walker. On the other, although the empirical problem (in the field and in the laboratory) is not nearly so bad as the hypothesis suggests, the empirical problem is nevertheless painfully real. The assurance contract warrants testing.

How to Observe Motives

In devising a test of the assurance contract, the problem I initially faced was to determine the empirical status of my hypothesis that Prisoner's Dilemmas are conjunctions of free rider and assurance problems. If a person does not contribute to a public goods project, how would we ever know what her reason was? And does her reason for withholding actually matter, or is this merely a distinction without a difference? The task was to design an experiment in which the two different kinds of withholding did not *look* the same.

Surprisingly enough, a suitably modified Isaac-Walker design can do this quite well. My method was to introduce a *provision point* into the Isaac-Walker design such that the good at stake became a *step good*—a good that cannot be provided at all until total contributions reached a certain critical level. Consider what happens if the provision point is set at 100 percent of the group's total endowment. In that case, free riding is impossible. If any subject withholds even a single token, then neither he nor anyone else can receive the group good. Because free riding is impossible, there is no rational fear of being taken advantage of—hence no exploitation problem. Rational subjects have only two reasons to withhold: the assurance problem and failure to understand the incentive structure. Alternatively, suppose we combine the 100 percent provision point with a money-back guarantee (i.e., a guarantee that contributions to the public exchange will be returned if the provision point is not met). In that case, contribution is a dominant strategy. Barring irrationality, failure to understand the situation would be the only reason for not contributing. Hence, the presence of assurance problems in the former case and their absence in the latter should account for any significant difference between contribution levels with and without the money-back guarantee. (Note that there are no honest holdouts in these experiments; all subjects make more money from mutual contribution than they do from mutual withholding.) Thus, we can infer the empirical significance of the assurance problem and can distinguish this significance from that of free rider problems and failures to understand.

Besides indicating the magnitude of the assurance problem, the modified Isaac-Walker design will also help us test, under laboratory conditions, the empirical effect the money-back guarantee has on the voluntary contributions mechanism for funding public goods provision. Hence it constitutes a test of the economic theory presented in Chapter 4 and, to a lesser extent, a test of the money-back guarantee as an economic policy. I discuss the distinction between theory tests and policy tests and report on two modified Isaac-Walker designs in later sections. First, however, I detail the results of the two other laboratory research projects of which I am aware that also bear on the efficacy of the money-back guarantee and on the assurance problem's significance in public goods contexts. On the basis of these four studies, which to my knowledge presently exhaust the experimental literature on the subject of money-back guarantees in the context of public goods production, I draw conclusions about the conditions under which assurance contracts might be effective.

Analyzing the Data

Bagnoli and McKee

Bagnoli and McKee (forthcoming) specifically sought to test the efficacy of a money-back guarantee in eliciting contributions in a public goods situation. Their groups consisted of either 5 subjects (seven groups in all) or 10 subjects (two groups in all), with subjects having individual endowments ranging between 7 and 16 tokens. The decision space was continuous; i.e., subjects were allowed to contribute whatever portion of their endowment they desired. The production function was binary; i.e., the group good was exactly 25 tokens if the provision point was met and nothing otherwise. In the event of failure, contributions were returned to those who made them. The group good was divided among subjects according to a pre-set pattern. In some experiments, the division was equal. In two of the 5-person experiments, subjects received from 1 to 10 tokens as their share of the group good. (This range was present within as well as across experiments, with individual endowments and valuations, as well as number of subjects, being common knowledge.) In all cases, the provision point was 12.5 tokens. (Subjects were allowed to contribute fractions of tokens.) The experiment consisted of 14 periods.

The seven 5-person groups met or exceeded the provision point in 85 of 98 periods (14 periods in each of seven experiments). Total contributions were within a half token of the provision point in 75 of 98 cases. Of the seven small groups, five earned 95 or more of the theoretical maximum for all 14 periods taken together. (The theoretical maximum is the sum of individual incomes, plus the total value of the public good produced, minus the minimum cost of reaching the provision point.) Five of seven groups actually attained the theoretical maximum over the last five periods and a sixth was very close. The two 10-person groups met the provision point in 17 of 28 periods. They were at 95 percent efficiency over the last five periods, although it took longer for the pattern of contributions to converge on an equilibrium.

An earlier draft of Bagnoli and McKee's paper concluded that their design achieved this striking level of efficiency by eliminating free rider problems. But what is interesting is that their design did not solve the free rider problem at all; rather, it induced public goods provision in spite of free rider problems. Their conclusion now says that "there are potential 'natural' institutions which are capable of efficient private provision of public or collective goods" (forthcoming, p. 14). The new phrasing does not mention the free rider problem. This is as it should be, for the most pertinent feature of Bagnoli and McKee's "natural" institution seems to be its money-back guarantee as a solution to the assurance problem. Unfortunately, we cannot be certain of this. The extent to which solving the assurance problem leads subjects to contribute in this experimental design remains unclear. For our purposes, it would have been ideal if the Bagnoli and McKee experiments had incorporated a control for the money-back variable. As it is, we do not know how much subjects would have contributed in this environment if they had not had a money-back guarantee. Hence, we have no way of knowing how much the money-back guarantee helped.

Dawes, Orbell, Simmons, and Van de Kragt

Dawes, et al. (1986), explore how well contributions are promoted by two devices: the *money-back guarantee* and *enforced fairness*. The first device returns contributions to those who made them if the group fails to meet its provision point. This solves the assurance problem. The second device requires contributions from those who did not contribute if the group succeeds in meeting its provision point. This solves the free rider problem, albeit nonvoluntarily.

Dawes, et al., hypothesized that contributions are better promoted by enforced fairness. Their rationale is this: The success of the money-back guarantee can be undermined by people's *expectation* that it will succeed. As subjects become more confident that the money-back mechanism will succeed, free riding comes to seem less risky, for it seems increasingly likely that their own contribution is not needed. Thus, the more the money-back mechanism succeeds, the more reason subjects have to withhold. In contrast, as subjects gain more confidence in enforced fairness, the assurance problem becomes less troublesome, for it seems increasingly likely that their own contribution will be sufficient (and the design rules out free riding). So the more the enforced fairness mechanism succeeds, the less reason subjects have to withhold.

Groups in these experiments consisted of seven subjects, each endowed with $5. Their task was to decide individually whether to contribute their endowment to the group project. The decision space was binary insofar as contributions between zero and $5 were not possible. The production technology was also binary. Each subject received $10 if the provision point was met and nothing otherwise. In the money-back dilemma, contributions were returned if the provision point was not met. The free rider problem remained, but the assurance problem had been eliminated. In the enforced fairness dilemma, noncontributors had $5 taken from them if the provision point was met. (In effect, there are no noncontributors when enforced fairness succeeds; enforced fairness is enforced unanimity.) The assurance problem remained, because those who contributed voluntarily would lose their money if the provision point was not met. But the free rider problem had been eliminated. Two provision points were examined. The first required $15, i.e., three of seven people to contribute. The second required $25, i.e., five of seven. These experiments consisted of a single period. The process was not iterated. As a control, *full dilemmas*, having neither money-back nor enforced fairness features, were also run with provision points.

Table 6.1
Three Kinds of Dilemmas in Dawes, et al. (percentage of subjects contributing)

	Provision Point = 3	Provision Point = 5
Full dilemma	51	64
Money-back dilemma	61	65
Enforced Fairness dilemma	86	93

As Table 6.1 shows, contributions in the Dawes, et al., study were substantially higher in the enforced fairness dilemma than in the full dilemma. Dawes, et al., concluded there was no statistically significant difference between full and money-back half dilemmas: "There is no ambiguity whatever about the success of the money-back guarantee device for eliciting contributions compared with the success of the enforced contribution device: the enforced contribution is superior" (1986, p. 1183). They also conclude that "Fear of loss through contributing is not the critical motivation underlying defection" (p. 1183).

Regarding their conclusion about the insignificance of the difference between full and money-back dilemmas, we might note that the observed difference in the experiments with three-person provision points would have become statistically significant had the difference been replicated over a modest number of further trials. We might also note that if instead of looking at individual contributions, we look at the proportion of groups meeting the provision point, we get a slightly different picture. That is, 11 of 20 groups met their provision point in the full dilemma, whereas 11 of 14 met their provision point in the money-back dilemma.

Regarding the difference found by Dawes, et al., between

money-back and enforced fairness dilemmas, their inference that fear of loss is not a critical motivation contradicts my hypothesis that the assurance problem is a major component of the public goods problem. But I believe their inference is invalid for the following reasons. First, enforced fairness does not function only by eliminating the chance to free ride. It also reduces the fear of loss by making it impossible for others to free ride. The design does not rule out the possibility that reducing fear in this way plays a critical role in the success of enforced fairness. Second, in the enforced fairness dilemma, unlike in the full or money-back dilemmas, there was no reason at all to fear that one's contribution would be wasted by virtue of being redundant. (Under the enforced fairness regime, when a subject's contribution is redundant, it would have been collected anyway, so it is not wasted in the way that redundant contributions are wasted in the money-back regime.) Thus, there are two ways in which the enforced fairness device reduced fear, while the alternatives did not, and both ways might reasonably be supposed to help the enforced fairness device to elicit contributions. Dawes, et al., conclude that the superiority of the enforced fairness device shows that fear of loss is not a critical motivational factor, but this conclusion is a non sequitur.

With respect to their claim that enforced fairness is the superior fundraising mechanism, an obvious problem is that enforced fairness is not a voluntary mechanism at all. We should not be too surprised that fundraising efforts are more likely to succeed when backed up by the threat of force. Suppose our faculty club wishes to raise money for the purpose of expanding the local museum. In one scenario, we agree to raise half a million dollars in order to get a matching grant from a large corporation, on the understanding that we will return faculty contributions if we fail to reach the half-million-dollar target. In an alternative scenario, we say we will try to raise a half million voluntarily, and if we succeed we will seize the other half million from faculty members who have not contributed yet. Even if enforced fairness is more effective, it raises rather urgent questions: How do we get that kind of power, and what gives us the right to use it in that way?

Moreover, aside from questions of legitimacy and problems in implementation, the conclusion that enforced fairness is superior does not follow from the data in the first place. In the Dawes, et al., design, the efficient levels of contributions were $15 (3 out of 7) and $25 (5 out of 7) respectively for the full dilemma. Because redundant contributions were wasted, efficiency was reduced by any contributions made in excess of these figures. The same is true of the money-back dilemma. In the enforced fairness dilemma, however, efficiency was not reduced by excess contributions—$35 was an efficient level of investment, because meeting the provision point meant that $35 was taken in any event. Obviously, this level of investment was not likely to be approached by the money-back mechanism; matching the contribution levels of enforced fairness (i.e., 86 percent and 93 percent) would have required people in the money-back experiments to throw their money away. (Subjects would not be certain they were throwing their money away, which mitigates my criticism, but they would be aware of the possibility.) When we consider that the efficient contribution levels in the money-back experiments were 43 percent and 71 percent respectively, rather than 100 percent, the actual money-back contribution levels of 61 percent and 65 percent begin to look respectable, to say the least. Dawes, et al., find "no ambiguity whatever" in the superiority of enforced fairness, but the results seem decidedly ambiguous to me.

Dawes, et al., hypothesized that the efficacy of the money-back guarantee would be undermined by the expectation of its success. This is true in their design. But perhaps real-world money-back guarantees are not subject to the same kind of undermining. In their design, increasing expectation of success also increased the expectation that one's contribution would be wasted, for there were two ways for it to be spent in vain. Both undercontribution and overcontribution entailed wasted investment in their design. Thus, the expectation of success not only creates a free rider problem—as it might do in the real world—but creates an assurance problem as well, which seems unrealistic.

Isaac, Schmidtz, and Walker

Mark Isaac, David Schmidtz, and James Walker (1989), hereafter ISW, used four-person groups, each person initially being endowed with 62 tokens. Each subject had a continuous decision space—i.e., each could contribute zero, 62, or any whole number of tokens in between. The value of the public good was $G(x) = 1.2x$ if the provision point was met and zero otherwise. The left side of the equation says that G, the value of the public good, is a function of x, the sum of individual contributions. The right side of the equation, the function's specific form, says that x is multiplied by 1.2 in its transformation into G. If the sum of individual contributions is two dollars, for example, and if two dollars meets or exceeds the provision point, then the value of the public good produced is two dollars and forty cents. This value is divided equally among subjects, so that, for example, if the sum of individual contributions is two dollars, then each of the four subjects receives one-fourth of G, which in this case is sixty cents. Because the public good production function is linear (i.e., since the number 1.2 is a constant) and continuous for all values of x that meet the provision point, there is no possibility of contributions being wasted by virtue of being redundant. (I.e., because 1.2 is greater than 1 and constant for all values of x, there is no possibility of overcontributing.) If the provision point is not met, contributions are returned in the money-back experiments and are not returned (i.e., are simply wasted) in the experimental controls, which lack the guarantee.

Three different provision points (high, medium, and low) were used. The high provision point (HPP = 248) represents 100 percent of the group's endowment. Thus, the HPP treatment eliminated the free rider problem. The HPP *money-back* experiments eliminated both free rider and assurance problems. The medium provision point (MPP = 216) represented the number of tokens sufficient to produce a return of at least 65 cents to each subject, thus ensuring that a given subject could contribute all 62 tokens and still make a profit if the provision point was met. The low provision point (LPP = 108) presented a provision level such that any subject making a contribution in excess of 32 tokens was not assured of earning a return worth more than 32 tokens even if the provision point was met. Thus, a subject contemplating a contribution of more than half his income had an assurance problem even given the money-back guarantee.

Subjects knew in advance that the experiment would run for ten periods. In early periods, there was a pronounced tendency for individual contributions to be approximately one-fourth of the provision point. (ISW call this a "focal point" contribution, a level of contribution that seems "obvious." See ISW, 1989, p. 223.) Table 6.2 pools data from eighteen experiments, six with each provision point. In keeping with the convention of Isaac, Walker, and Thomas (1984), the individual contributions are separated into five size categories ranging from zero to 62.

Table 6.2
First-Period Individual Contributions in Isaac, Schmidtz and Walker, No Money-Back Guarantee (number of subjects contributing)

Size Range of Contributions:	Low Provision Pt. (focal pt. = 27)	Medium Provision Pt. (focal pt. = 54)	High Provision Pt. (focal pt. = 62)
0	1	3	8
1-20	3	3	0
21-41	15	2	1
42-61	2	12	3
62	3	2	12
Total	24	24	24

Notice that contribution levels increased in proportion to increases in the provision point level. This is rather odd, because one would intuitively think that assurance problems would become worse as the provision point rises. Table 6.2 suggests that provision points may have served as focal points in early periods. As the experiment progressed, however, contributions usually collapsed completely. Table 6.3 shows the end-period result.

Table 6.3
Final-Period Individual Contributions in Isaac, Schmidtz, and Walker, No Money-Back Guarantee (number of subjects contributing)

Size Range of Contributions:	Low Provision Pt.	Medium Provision Pt.	High Provision Pt.
0	19	20	19
1-20	1	0	1
21-41	3	0	0
42-61	0	3	0
62	1	1	4
Total	24	24	24

On the other hand, in 3 of the 18 experiments (one for each provision point), contributions remained at higher levels than ever observed before in the general Isaac-Walker design. (The four contributions of 62 tokens in Table 6.3's HPP data pool, for instance, all came from a single experiment.) ISW's conclusion is that without the money-back guarantee, the introduction of a provision point can dramatically increase contribution levels in a few cases, but generally does not succeed and probably makes matters worse (1989, p. 228). Thus, introducing the provision point itself made a difference, the extent of which depended upon the contribution level at which the provision point was set.

ISW found that Pareto-superior Nash equilibria tended to collapse to Pareto-inferior Nash equilibria.[2] This was true with and without the possibility of "cheap riding" (i.e., contributing only the minimal amount necessary to reach the provision point, given the expected pattern of contribution of the other members of the group). It does not appear to be dominance as such that causes the underprovision of public goods (ISW, 1989, p. 229). Subjects' reasons for contributing are more complicated (and often considerably less rational) than that.

Introducing the money-back guarantee, however, made a substantial difference. Overall, success in meeting provision points went from 45 out of 180 to 93 out of 180 periods when a money-back guarantee was added. Figures 6.1, 6.2, and 6.3 compare average contribution levels for money-back versus no-money-back treatments on a per-period basis, for each of the three provision points.

Figure 6.1
Mean number of tokens contributed in Isaac, Schmidtz & Walker high provision point

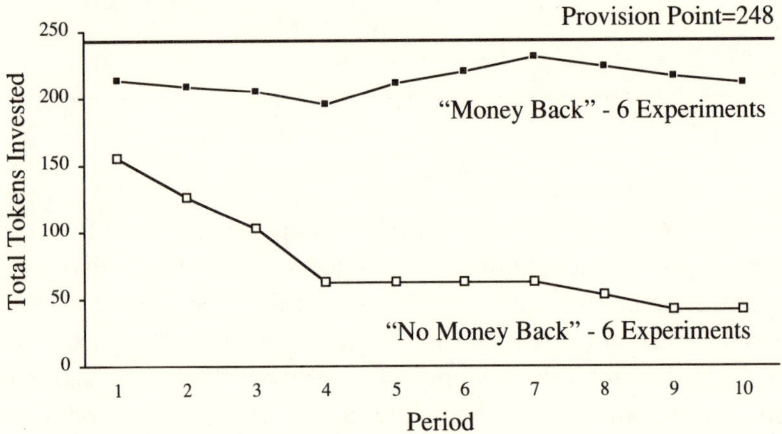

Figure 6.2
Mean number of tokens contributed in Isaac, Schmidtz & Walker medium provision point

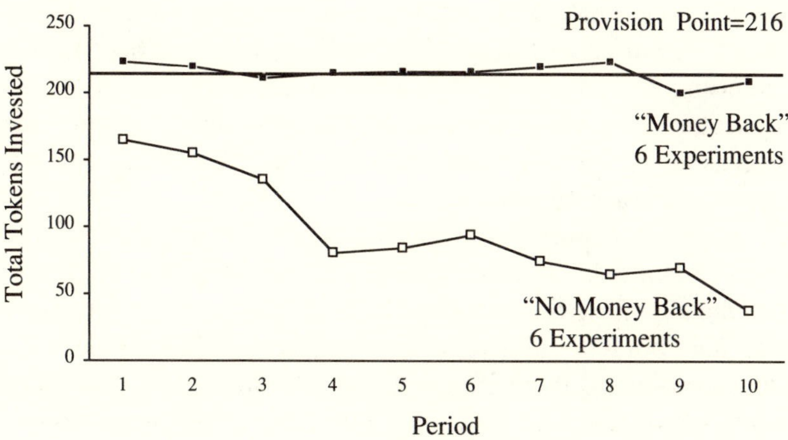

Figure 6.3
Mean number of tokens contributed in Isaac, Schmidtz & Walker low provision point

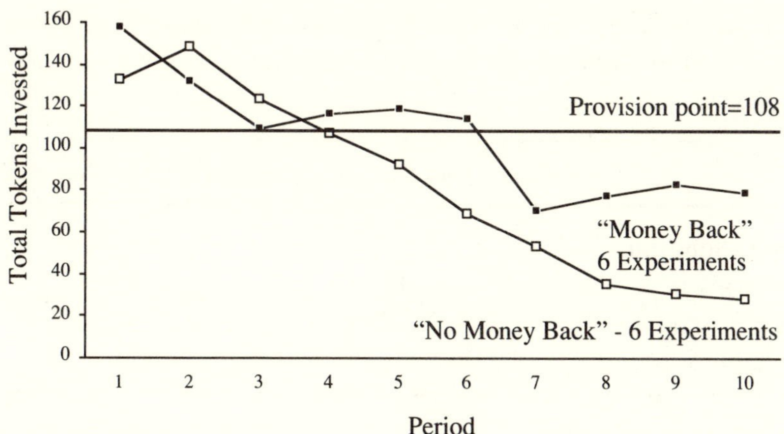

Source: R. Mark Isaac, David Schmidtz, and James M. Walker. "The Assurance Problem in a Laboratory Market." Public Choice, 62 (1989). Reprinted by permission of Kluwer Academic Publishers.

These observations suggest that the assurance problem is observationally distinguishable from the free rider problem and that it is a significant part of public goods problems. Further, the money-back guarantee that solves the assurance problem in theory also makes an empirical difference. Especially, note Figure 6.1. With or without the guarantee, the 248-token provision point renders exploitation and free riding impossible. The assurance problem is the sole reason for the difference between the money-back and no-money-back contribution levels.

For practical purposes, imposing a provision point without the guarantee is a risky strategy. (Also, imagine people's reaction as you try to explain to them that you have decided not to produce any of the good but will not give their money back either.) Imposing a provision point together with a money-back guarantee appears to be a rather good idea, certainly better than simply asking for contributions. Table 6.4 shows the experimental success of the money-back guarantee in meeting provision points compared with that of the no money-back experimental controls.

Table 6.4
Comparing Dawes, et al., with Isaac, Schmidtz and Walker, and Bagnoli and McKee (number of periods in which groups met provision points)

	Money-Back Guarantee	No Money-Back Guarantee
Isaac, Schmidtz, & Walker	93/180	45/180
Dawes, et al.	11/14	11/20
Bagnoli & McKee	85/98	no data

In the HPP money-back experiments, contributing 62 tokens was a dominant strategy. Contributing anything less was unquestionably a mistake, minimizing the subject's own income as well as that of the group. Nevertheless, it happened. Figure 6.1 shows the gap between the 248-token provision point and the line representing data from the money-back experiments. If all subjects had played their dominant strategies, there would have been no gap. In fact, however, in 56 out of 240 individual decisions made in the six 10-period HPP experiments, subjects did not play their dominant strategy. Why? I have no truly satisfying answer, but we should note that nearly half of these failures to contribute occurred within a single experiment—one in which subjects reported responding to the group's initial failure by lowering their own bids either in frustration or in an attempt to prompt the others to action. It also might have been important that those who irrationally made suboptimal contributions in the HPP money-back experiments continued to earn an income of 62 tokens. (In contrast, those who contributed amounts between 0 and 62 tokens in the no guarantee HPP experiment lost their contributions, and the loss quickly taught them not to repeat their mistake.) Perhaps some subjects considered an income of 62 cents per period perfectly satisfactory and for this reason felt no need to examine the possibility that contributing 62 tokens was actually a dominant strategy. This raises another question. It was assumed (at least by me) that a money-back guarantee would solve assurance problems without systematically affecting the amount of suboptimality attributable to simple failure to understand the game. However, if a person could be hurt by his or her own misunderstanding in one game, but could not be hurt in the same way in the other game, then perhaps my assumption is unwarranted. Perhaps there would be a difference in the person's tendency to learn from mistakes. If so, then this suggests that the gap between money-back and no-money-back experiments may understate the magnitude of the assurance problem. (Of course, because my main conclusion here is that the assurance problem is empirically significant, this possibility is not a threat.)

One thing the ISW design does not do is allow subjects to observe each other's contribution within any given period. To the extent that they care about what other subjects are doing, they must respond to other subjects on the basis of cumulative information from past periods. In a given period, there was no way for them to learn about other subjects' intentions or to signal their own. In this respect, the ISW design is a poor model of the telethon approach to fundraising, for example, because contributors to a telethon scheme have access to continuously updated information on what other contributors have so far pledged. Frequently, they also have information about "challenge pledges"—contributions that have been promised pending the materialization of a certain level of contributions from others. (The fire department might challenge the police department, for example.) Of course, the purpose of ISW's experiments (from my point of view) was to verify the empirical significance of the assurance problem, not to test the efficiency of telethons. The primary intent was to test theory, not policy. We will discuss the difference between tests of theory and tests of policy after we take note of recently completed experiments that do provide information about the efficiency of telethon approach.

Further Applications of the Isaac-Walker Design

Robert Dorsey (unpublished) employed the basic design and incentive structure of ISW. Dorsey's design, however, incorporates a major advance. It modifies the decisionmaking environment so as to determine whether the decisionmaking process is sensitive to temporal factors and to the associated changes in the kind of information people have when making decisions. Dorsey's design gave subjects three minutes within each period to enter or update their contributions to the public exchange, in light of changing information about what the rest of the group had so far contributed in that period. This added time element reflects the kind of information and opportunity to update contributions that decisionmakers often have.

A second advantage of Dorsey's design over ISW's is that the extra information with which it provides subjects can alleviate assurance problems to a degree without resorting to provision points combined with money-back guarantees. This is so because a subject can easily see, given what other subjects have contributed, how much he or she can afford to contribute and still be assured of making a profit. What is required to solve the assurance problem is a condition that subjects can only add to previous pledges, not subtract from them. When subjects can add to or subtract from previous pledges, the assurance problem is present in full force.

By adding a provision point, ISW also introduced a focal point, which meant that they had to control for the possibility that the focal point rather than the money-back guarantee caused the rise in contribution levels. Because Dorsey's design dispensed with the need for a provision point, this control problem did not arise for him. Nevertheless, although Dorsey was able to design a fundraising mechanism that solved the assurance problem without introducing a focal point, he still wanted to test the effect of adding a provision point to what he called a "real-time" environment—one with a time element that permits subjects to update contributions. Unlike ISW, who found that the provision point had a real but equivocal effect on contribution levels in the simultaneous game, Dorsey found that incorporating provision points in the real-time game had a substantial positive effect on contribution levels.

Dorsey contrasted the increase-only rule to a rule by which subjects could either increase or decrease commitments made previously in that period. In effect, the increase-or-decrease rule rendered pledges nonbinding. In such an environment, the temporal aspect of the real-time game does nothing to solve the assurance problem, even for "last second" contributors. As we would expect, Dorsey found that in this environment, contribution levels were much lower, sometimes collapsing entirely at the end of the three-minute period.

Table 6.5 reflects data gathered by Dorsey from sixteen experiments with the increase-only rule and eight experiments with the increase-or-decrease rule. In each treatment, half the experiments were run with no provision point and half with a provision point of 108 tokens (equal to the low provision point of ISW).

Table 6.5
The Effect of Real Time in Dorsey (contributions as a median percentage of groups' total endowments; mean percentages shown in parentheses)

	Increase-Only Rule	Increase-or-Decrease Rule
No provision point	15.7 (20.24)	8.1 (11.53)
Provision point = 108	44.4 (34.76)	26.6 (26.98)

Source: Robert E. Dorsey, "The Voluntary Contributions Mechanism with Real Time Revisions." Unpublished. Reprinted by permission of the author.

What we see is that adding a provision point in the real-time environment dramatically increases median contribution levels. (Even under the increase-or-decrease rule, the median contribution level was 26.6 percent with the provision point but only 8.1 percent without.) We also see that contribution levels are significantly higher under the increase-only rule than under the increase-or-decrease rule. Median contributions were nearly twice as high under the increase-only rule. Moreover, the real-time element itself makes a difference. Table 6.6 compares the data from Dorsey with data from ISW. ISW ran six experiments with 108 token provision points and another six experiments that also included a money-back guarantee against failure to meet the 108-token provision point. The median percentage of total tokens contributed in these experiments is presented in Table 6.6 for purposes of comparison.

Table 6.6
Comparing Dorsey with Isaac, Schmidtz, and Walker (contributions as a median percentage of groups' total endowments)

	Increase-Only Rule	Increase-or-Decrease Rule	ISW	ISW (money-back)
Provision Pt. = 108	44.4	26.6	30.2	42.7

Dorsey notes the following about the ISW results: "Isaac, Schmidtz, and Walker, using identical parameters but without real time adjustments, reported that with a provision point of 108, only one experiment out of six achieved the provision point after the fourth period. With the real time environment, the provision point was reached at least once after the fourth period in eight out of 12 of the ten-period experiments" (Dorsey, unpublished, p. 16).

Dorsey's real-time game is a different game. It has different rules, induces real people to play different strategies, and leads to different results. I once argued that the temporal factor could induce people to contribute more to a public goods project funded by assurance contract than they otherwise might (Schmidtz, 1987a, pp. 497ff). As David Friedman noted in response, my argument left open the possibility that people in a real-time situation might choose to wait until the last second. In the limit, everyone waits until the last second—thus, no one has any information about what anyone else is planning to do. "We all make our decisions in ignorance of what the rest are doing. We are back in the simultaneous game" (Friedman, 1987, p. 519). Dorsey's experiments, however, show that this is not how the temporal factor works.

How, then, do we explain the fact that contribution levels rose when intra-period decisions were made in real time? For one thing, the real-time element allows subjects to see whether total contributions are below the provision point at any particular moment during the period, while there is still time to do something about it. If we think of total contributions as being like a missile launched at the provision point, then the temporal factor allows players to use their contributions to guide the total toward the provision point. Without the temporal factor that allows subjects to adjust contributions, total contributions are like a ballistic missile. After the initial decision, no further control is possible. The analogy breaks down, however, when we use the increase-or-decrease rule, for with that rule, previous contributions can be withdrawn at a moment's notice. Thus, individual subjects have no firm information about what adjustments will actually be required to meet the provision point as the period draws to a close.

I also suspect the increase-only format effectively converted the intra-period game from a one-shot Prisoner's Dilemma to something that could be played as an iterated Prisoner's Dilemma. That is, a subject could contribute one penny, then step back until total contributions rose to a level sufficient to repay a one-penny contribution (say, four cents). Then the subject could contribute one more penny and when total contributions rose to a level adequate as a reciprocation for the subject's two-cent contribution, take this as a cue to initiate another round by contributing one more, and so on. When Dorsey sequentially plotted intra-period contributions, the resulting curve in some cases showed just the series of regular small steps we would expect from such a strategy (Dorsey, unpublished).

Whether this kind of strategy characteristically underlies the success of telethon fundraisers is far from clear, but it may be a part of it. Moreover, aside from the aspect of reciprocity permitted by the real-time environment, there is also the prospect of being able to make a decision with an assurance about the minimum level of total contributions one may expect, and this presumably is a big factor in both the Dorsey experiments and in the telethons that these experiments model. (I discuss the moral status of reciprocity in Chapter 7.)

Dorsey's results also have a significance that goes beyond their implications as a model of telethon fundraisers. Consider, for example, how it might be used to model negotiations over disarmament. (Let me stress at the beginning, however, that I have no more than a layman's knowledge of cold war politics. The point of the following is only to illustrate the practical applications of

Dorsey's model. Moreover, the example may strike the reader as out of date, but it was a fair description of the status quo for several decades.)[3] The Soviets had an approach to disarmament (circa 1988) that suggests an attempt to capitalize on the incentives associated with the real-time element. They apparently were taking unilateral steps to disarm and demilitarize. As the United States government liked to stress, it is indeed true that these steps were very small. But small steps were precisely what the situation called for. The Soviets had a very pressing assurance problem and could not be expected to take larger steps unilaterally. My reaction as a game theorist was that, if the cuts were genuine, then the United States should respond by cutting its military strength by slightly more than the Soviets cut theirs, so as to put the onus on the Soviets to maintain the momentum. To respond by saying that the United States cannot cut its arms stockpiles as long as the Soviets maintain an edge seems disingenuous; if the United States wants the Soviets to drastically reduce their stockpiles, it must must offer them something. The Soviets may have an edge, but it is also true that both sides have more missiles than is healthy. If the United States wants the Soviets to cut back on conventional forces, it should get things started by making a small cut (but large enough to be recognizable as such) in its own conventional forces.

One major obstacle to successful negotiations in this area is the problem of monitoring compliance. It is relatively easy to ensure that a given missile has been rendered inoperative; the big problem is to ensure that replacements are not secretly being built. But notice the structure of this monitoring problem. The problem involves making sure that we are not playing an increase-or-decrease game. What we need is an assurance that the only available moves will be subtractions from the arms stockpile. Covert additions to stockpiles must be ruled out. The game will not run smoothly until we are in a position to play by a decrease-only rule with incentive properties equivalent to those of Dorsey's increase-only rule for monetary contributions.[4]

For public goods problems involving a need to secure monetary contributions, a logical next step in the line of research begun by Isaac and Walker would be to compare a real-time provision point environment to one that added a money-back guarantee in the event the provision point was not met. Although the provision point induced greater contributions in the Dorsey experiments, it also featured an assurance problem, because to initiate the incremental process of building up to the provision point, subjects had to accept the risk of never reaching it, thereby wasting whatever they had contributed. Solving this assurance problem with a money-back guarantee resulted in an increase of nearly 50 percent in median contributions (from 30.2 to 42.7 percent of total endowment) in ISW. Combining the real-time and money-back features might lead to still higher contribution levels.

Theory Tests and Policy Tests

What can we infer about the role of experimental economics in assessing the merits of assurance contracts? Experimental methods can be used to test both economic theory and economic policy.[5] But testing descriptive theory and testing prescriptive policy are two different things. We must be careful not to confuse them, because experimental methods serve different functions in these two roles and are subject to different problems. The function of a test of an economic prescription is to shift the burden of proof onto those who believe that a certain policy will have different effects in the rest of the world than it does in the laboratory. The result of such a test is by no means decisive, but if the policy does not work in the laboratory, this should at least lead us to reexamine our reasons for prescribing the policy.

In contrast, the intent of a test of descriptive theory is to confirm or disconfirm a theory insofar as it yields testable predictions when applied to the experimental design. This is not to say that single tests are typically decisive. In fact, they seldom are. The point, rather, is that a descriptive theory can be confirmed or disconfirmed in a way that a prescriptive policy cannot.

For example, we might have a descriptive theory that people are exclusively self-interested. Or we might prescribe a policy of always treating people as if they were exclusively self-interested when we are trying to implement efficient mechanisms for providing public services in large urban communities. The data discussed in preceding sections weigh heavily against the theory that people are exclusively self-interested. We may not want to say that the data decisively refute the theory, but the theory is certainly misleading in a variety of laboratory situations in which people are called on to engage in collective action. The results do not show that the prescriptive policy is false, however, or even that it is bad policy. Following the policy might very well yield the results it was intended to yield when followed in the particular kind of situation for which it was prescribed.

The pitfall to avoid in policy tests is careless extrapolation from the laboratory to situations that are different in kind. Laboratory simulations of large-scale policy problems are inevitably unrealistic. The possibility that some of the disanalogies will be relevant is inescapable. This is an empirical problem, inherent in any field of empirical research. But policy prescriptions are not intended to apply to laboratory situations. The laboratory policy test must be understood as essentially a simulation of the situation for which the policy was really proposed.

In contrast, the danger of inappropriate extrapolation does not arise in the same way for tests of theory. Disconfirmation in the laboratory is disconfirmation, period. We do not need to know if the experimental design is realistic—we just need to know if the theory applies to the design. One may suspect that the theory yields true predictions in other situations, but in any event, following up this suspicion requires one to modify the theory (preferably not in an ad hoc way) so that it is no longer systematically disconfirmed by what has been observed in the laboratory. Laboratory situations are real situations involving real people and real money. Theory tests in the laboratory are not "dry runs" in the way policy tests are. They are not merely simulations. Laboratory situations are themselves situations for which theories can have testable implications. Whether or not they simulate the real world, they are capable of disconfirming a theory, provided the theory yields testable implications when applied to them.

The possibility remains, however, that the theory will not

apply at all in this sense. This is the real problem with tests of economic theory. If, for example, subjects receive unintelligible instructions, or if the monetary incentives are insignificant, then most economic theories will say nothing about what behavior we should expect to observe. The problem will not be that the situation is unrealistic. (Confused subjects and insignificant monetary rewards are features of many real-world situations.) The problem will simply be that the theory has no testable implications under such circumstances.

The Verdict on Assurance Contracts

Can contractual solutions to the assurance problem generate adequate funding for public goods production? Laboratory results are promising but inconclusive. Solving the assurance problem makes a substantial difference, but even a design that made optimal contributions a dominant strategy failed to elicit optimal contributions consistently. Still, the laboratory data yielded one interesting result that is clear: Dominance per se is not what leads people to pick one strategy over another. The decision procedures people actually employ are much harder to characterize than that. Subjects contribute to public goods projects even when noncontribution is a dominant strategy. Their contributions, however, tend to be suboptimal because of free rider, exploitation, and assurance problems. Also, some subjects probably fail to make optimal contributions simply because they fail to comprehend the request.

As a policy tool, money-back guarantees generally ought to be incorporated into attempts to fund public goods production by voluntary contributions. Of course, in many cases, it is fairly obvious that a certain fundraising effort will meet its target in any event. In these cases, there is no point in complicating the issue with a superfluous guarantee. In other cases, it is not obvious at all that the target will be met. For these cases, the money-back guarantee should be used, but the provision point must be chosen with great care. It must be set at a level of funding that could reasonably be considered both necessary and sufficient for the good in question to be successfully produced. In addition to the obvious point that a necessary and sufficient level of funding is the amount of funding we want in the first place, a provision point set at such a level will be taken more seriously by prospective contributors. The disadvantage of setting a provision point at all is that if it is not met, the fundraisers end up with nothing. But if the provision point is set so that a funding level below it would be inadequate anyway, the disadvantage may not matter. When there is no natural provision point and the adequacy of funding is strictly a matter of degree, then the task for fundraisers is simply to maximize revenue. The evidence is that the combination of a well-chosen provision point and a money-back guarantee increases expected revenue. It does not guarantee increased revenues, however. Contributors, not fundraisers, get the guarantee.

Of course, many people feel that the provision of critically important public goods must not be left to chance, and hence, such goods must be produced coercively. I understand this feeling—I often feel the same way. But there is irony here: Isaac and Walker (1988) have shown that the higher the marginal rate of return from individual contributions, the higher contribution levels tend to be. This is consistent with the impression that, historically, people contribute vastly larger amounts (in terms of money and voluntary service) to the military in times of war than in times of peace. Public goods projects as important as national defense, at least during times when the importance of such projects is most obvious, tend to be those least in need of coercive support.

Thus, one should not conclude that coercion is justified or even desirable merely because the good at stake is crucial. Still, interesting questions remain. Chapter 4 discussed conditions under which Jane might rationally contribute to AIDS research. But when, if ever, is she morally obligated to contribute? When are we morally permitted to force her to contribute? These are the questions that will occupy us in Chapter 7.

7

The Morality of a Cooperative Society

We all have needs. Spurred by need, we act. We do not act in isolation, however, for we do not live in isolation. We live together. We pursue our own projects, but we also cross each other's paths in the process, sometimes for good, sometimes not. Thus, a person's pursuits sometimes have external effects (i.e., effects that spill over into the lives of the rest of us without our consent). External effects are often negative, but they can also be a boon. People who undertake to produce public goods (by defending their homeland, for instance) generate positive externalities; they benefit citizens in general, not just themselves. In light of the positive externalities at stake, when are we obligated to help produce public goods? When are others permitted to force us to help?

In this chapter I first outline a framework for answering these questions; I offer a conceptual analysis of property rights and characterize the ways in which public goods problems might override property rights. Second, I show how we might add normative content to that analytical framework; I canvas the various behavioral norms one might encounter in Prisoner's Dilemmas and evaluate their relative plausibility as moral norms. Third, I bring the framework to bear on questions about the nature and scope of our moral obligation to help produce public goods. Finally, I stake out parts of a more general theory of morality and use it to show how the analytical framework, when combined with a normative theory, can answer the question of when others are permitted to force us to help produce public goods. The more general theory of morality also supplies an underlying rationale both for property rights and for their moral limits in the face of public goods problems.

A Two-Part Analysis of Property Rights

Property rights, as I see them, are conjunctions of *prerogatives* and correlative *restrictions*.[1] To claim that I own a certain object is really to make two claims: First, I have the prerogative to use that object as I see fit, within limits. Second, other people do not have the prerogative to use that object as they see fit—there is a restriction against using the object without my permission, though this restriction also has limits. How shall we characterize the limits of prerogatives and restrictions? Borrowing a term from epistemology, let us say that restrictions and prerogatives are *defeated* if and when what normally suffices to justify them fails to do so in the particular case.

We have said that this chapter is concerned with two questions. When are you obligated to help produce public goods? When am I permitted to force you to help? We are now in a position to explain why these are two different questions. Insofar as public goods production depends on people giving up their property, it runs up against property rights. In doing so, it runs up against two different kinds of principles—prerogatives and restrictions. The prerogative component of property rights implies that you are not obligated to contribute. Thus, the question of when you *are* obligated to contribute your property is actually a question of when your prerogative is defeated. The correlative restriction implies it is not right to force you to contribute your property. Thus, the question of when others *may* force you to contribute your property is actually a question of when the restriction component of property rights is defeated. The defeat of the prerogative and the defeat of the restriction are two conceptually separate events. In terms of the moral borders around you, the line that separates what you can and cannot do with your property is conceptually distinguishable from the line that separates what other people can and cannot do with your property. Accordingly, the relocation of one border does not entail the relocation of the other. (This dualism of moral principles applies not only to property rights but also more generally to the conceptual distinction between what I ought to do and what I can be forced to do. For example, there are times when, say, failing to tell the truth is not my prerogative but when the restriction against forcing the truth out of me remains in full force.)

Now, let us consider how public goods problems might generate defeaters. (I should stress that the point here is simply to define the possibilities; for the moment, we leave open the question of whether rights are ever actually defeated.) The stakes involved in public goods problems are represented by the *cost-benefit* gap (which is equivalent to the R - c gap introduced in Chapter 4). The cost-benefit gap measures the difference between two quantities. The first is a person's benefit from a given level of public goods production. The second is the cost of the person's contribution towards providing the public good at that level. I analyze those defeaters to which public goods problems might give rise in terms of the sign and magnitude of the cost-benefit gap. Other kinds of social concerns may suggest other kinds of rights defeaters, but if there are rights defeaters associated with public goods problems, they will emerge from the factors that make it important to solve public goods problems in the first place, namely the costs and benefits of public goods production.

We may separate defeaters based on individual cost-benefit gaps from those based on a summation of cost-benefit gaps of the group as a whole. Because we may also distinguish prerogative defeaters from restriction defeaters, these two distinctions give rise to four conceptual categories. Any defeaters generated specifically by public goods problems will fall into one of these four categories. One's prerogative not to give up one's property for the sake of public goods production might be defeated by the magnitude of one's own cost-benefit gap or by that of the cost-benefit summation. (The former defeater is associated with considerations of fair play, the latter with considerations of beneficence.) Likewise, the restriction against forcing one to give up one's property might be defeated by the magnitude either of one's own cost-benefit gap or of the cost-benefit summation. (We might call the former defeater paternalistic and the latter redistributive.) In other words, a public good may be so valuable to me that I ought to help produce it, or it might be so valuable to others that I ought to help them produce it (whether or not it is also valuable to me). Likewise, a public good may be so valuable to me that others can permissibly force me to help produce it, or so valuable to others that they can permissibly force me to help produce it (whether or not it is also valuable to me).

These, then, are the four categories of defeaters relevant to public goods production. Again, this analytical framework leaves open whether each (or any) of these categories has members; it is meant to clarify such controversies rather than assume them away. To extract substantive normative conclusions from the framework, we must feed normative principles into it. Accordingly, the next two sections explore the normative foundations of property rights.

Reciprocity in Two-Person Games

In the absence of coercion, what should individual citizens do to help secure the net benefits of public goods production? To decide what people should do, we must first determine what their options are. Consider an ordinary "one-shot" Prisoner's Dilemma with two players. In such a situation, a *nonstrategic egoist* defects because his return (r) from a unit of contribution (c) would be less than one unit. A *nonstrategic altruist* cooperates because the return to the group (R) from his unit of contribution is more than one. In this simplest of Prisoner's Dilemmas, defection and cooperation are the only possible choices, and the marginal returns to the group and to the individuals involved are the only reasons the game presents for choosing between defection and cooperation.

Things become more complicated when the players engage in repeated play or when it becomes possible to adopt conditional strategies within the one-shot game. In particular, a third strategy becomes possible. A *reciprocator* will cooperate if and only if his partner is a cooperator. In a one-shot game where it is possible to make one's choice conditional on the choice of one's partner, a reciprocator will cooperate if his partner cooperates and will defect if his partner defects. In repeated play, if a reciprocator cannot make conditional choices within particular iterations of the game, then he will respond instead to his partner's play in the previous game, cooperating if his partner previously cooperated and defecting if his partner previously defected.

Interesting data on such strategies are readily available. Robert Axelrod has shown that reciprocity is extraordinarily effective at generating patterns of cooperation in two-person Prisoner's Dilemmas with repeated play. Axelrod invited professional game theorists to enter their favorite strategy in a computer tournament, where each strategy was matched against each of the others to see which would do best overall (1984, p. 20). In a series of tournaments, the more exploitive strategies consistently trailed the field.[2] As Axelrod puts it: "There is a single property which distinguishes the relatively high-scoring entries from the relatively low-scoring entries. This is the property of being *nice*, which is to say never being the first to defect" (1984, p. 33). Nice strategies outperformed more exploitive strategies by fostering the patterns of cooperation necessary for players to do well in repeated Prisoner's Dilemmas. The best strategies were those based on reciprocity. Reciprocal strategies are "nice." Reciprocators never defect first, but they do respond to other players' moves in kind. Defection is met with defection, cooperation with cooperation. Reciprocal strategies are agreeable to cooperative partners and punishing to exploitive partners.

Next, consider how pervasive the Prisoner's Dilemma game structure is. It applies (honest holdouts aside) not only to public goods problems but to ordinary exchanges of private goods as well.[3] For example, suppose I prefer Jane's apples to my fence posts, and Jane prefers my fence posts to her apples. If we exchange fence posts for apples, we will both be better off. But why should I give Jane my fence posts? Why generate positive externalities by making fence posts for apple-barons like Jane? Why not make fence posts only for myself, and when Jane has things I want, simply take them? For that matter, why make fence posts at all? If I want fence posts, why not take them as well? My consuming Jane's apples without paying for them will (at best) look like a negative externality to Jane, but why should I care?

As Demsetz points out, "A primary function of property rights is that of guiding incentives to achieve a greater internalization of externalities" (1967, p. 348). To internalize externalities is to increase the extent to which costs and benefits that would otherwise be externalities are instead borne by those who generate them. (Thus, for example, we could internalize the externality of pollution after the fact by forcing people to clean up after themselves, or before the fact by taxing the activities that cause pollution.) Ultimately, property rights make cooperative exchange possible, for when we see that we cannot simply take each other's possessions and that our own possessions cannot simply be taken from us, we can condition the terms of our respective offers. We can say that Jane's apples become mine if and only if my fence posts become hers.

One thing we should notice about this argument, however, is that it presumes that we can condition the terms of our exchange. It has to be feasible for Jane to insist that I give her fence posts as a condition of her giving me apples. Thus, enforced property rights make it possible for us to internalize externalities by providing the framework that gives us the scope to act as reciprocators. The framework allows Jane to hang on to her apples if she does not like the terms of my offer. But it is the reciprocity itself—not the property rights—that actually effects the internalization. Consider that if we find ourselves in a one-shot prisoner's dilemma where we must choose independently whether to cooperate or defect, we are in trouble. Our fence posts and apples may be our private property, but that fact is not enough. The truly crucial factor, our ability to condition our offers, is missing. Property rights enter the picture by giving agents the prerogative to condition their offers. Putting this prerogative to use, when conditions permit, is what internalizes externalities.

The following section argues that reciprocity is a fundamental moral norm. Subsequent sections use this conclusion to inject normative content into the previously developed conceptual framework so that we may flesh out the nature of prerogative defeaters associated with public goods problems.

Reciprocity in a Cooperative Society

Society, says John Rawls, is a cooperative venture for mutual advantage (1971, p. 4). My first premise—at least my first explicit premise—is that, all other things being equal, one candidate for the status of fundamental moral norm is superior to another along a critically important dimension if it is more conducive to the success of this cooperative venture. Superiority along this dimension may not always be decisive, but it surely counts for something, especially in a discussion of the moral norms pertaining to public goods production. Many deontologists believe that the morality of a norm turns on whether it can be universalized, but this raises a question as to how we decide whether a norm can be universalized. Because few norms can be ruled out on the grounds that universalizing them would be literally self-contradictory, deontologists also tend to consider whether a norm is pragmatically consistent with the flourishing of a kingdom of ends. I mention this to counter any impression that my first premise could be accepted only by utilitarians. The first premise is compatible with a variety of positions concerning exactly what the flourishing of society has to do with morality; it assumes only that being conducive to the success of cooperative society is, all other things equal, a good thing.

My second premise is factual: Individuals make decisions. (I leave open whether things other than individuals also make decisions.) In particular, individuals decide whether to abide by moral norms. Given the first premise, the second premise bears on what can count as a fundamental moral norm because it bears on what norms are conducive to cooperation. Because we choose norms for ourselves, *the norms that actually promote cooperation often differ from the norms that would promote cooperation if we were choosing norms for everyone*. This is so for the following reason: If by our actions we could effectively choose norms for everyone, we would not have to worry about how others act. (We would be able to treat the tendency to follow norms as a constant, ignoring the facts that this tendency varies with the incentives to follow the norms and that the incentives vary with the content of the norms.) In the real world, however, there is scarcely anything about which we need to worry more. Society is a cooperative venture, but not everyone seeking a share of the benefits of cooperation is a cooperator.

Thus, if Jane could choose which norm would be followed by everyone involved in our cooperative venture, nonstrategic altruism (i.e., contributing whenever overall welfare is thereby increased) would be a very plausible choice. The problem with nonstrategic altruism is caused not so much by the altruism as by the fact that the norm is nonstrategic. In particular, it fails to take into account that not everyone is a nonstrategic altruist. The benefit of such a strategy falls upon altruists and nonaltruists alike, often disproportionately upon nonaltruists, because they will change their strategies so as to tap the flow of benefits, and some will try to tap this flow for free. In this way, those who altruistically offer free apples to whoever can make good use of them encourage nonaltruists to become free riders. The kind of behavior that undermines cooperation can proliferate. The problem is not that Jane is unable or unwilling to follow a standard of nonstrategic altruism (although that may be true as well). Rather, others are unable or unwilling to resist exploiting Jane if she follows it.

Fortunately, nonstrategic altruism often is not the only alternative to free riding, and the tendency of nonstrategic altruism to foster free riding often can be avoided by adopting an alternative strategy. Specifically, morality can let Jane avoid encouraging others to free ride by letting her refuse to cooperate with others unless they also cooperate with her. It also gives her an incentive not to free ride—more precisely, it lets others give her this incentive—because it lets others refuse to cooperate with her unless she cooperates with them. In this way, reciprocity works through moral agents such as Jane to teach people not to expect opportunities to free ride—in short, to be (at least to this extent) moral agents themselves. Reciprocity helps control the access to those positive externalities that can otherwise bleed a cooperative society to death. And reciprocity simultaneously gives Jane and others an incentive to act as morality requires in the first place, namely, as dues-paying members of cooperative society.

Let me emphasize that I am not suggesting that reciprocal

norms are legitimate merely because adhering to them is typically rational from the viewpoint of individual agents in a cooperative venture. To illustrate the point that the collective viewpoint (so to speak) motivates the more calculating form of cooperation embodied in reciprocity, suppose we can capture the idea of the impersonal viewpoint in the metaphor of society as an organism. Further, suppose the social organism could "decide." For its own health, its decisions would take into account effects that were externalities from the viewpoints of its components. (For example, the social organism would choose for its components to give blood, because the benefits as well as the costs are internal to it as a decisionmaking unit.) However, the social organism's decisionmaking is in fact decentralized; its components are the decisionmakers. Moreover, these components are more or less intent on satisfying their own needs. Consequently, its health requires that its components *give each other* the incentive to take the positive external effects of their actions into account (for example, by giving free blood transfusions or other special treatment to those who have previously given blood). Reciprocity is a good idea from the social organism's viewpoint, not just from the viewpoints of its parts.

Some might think it implausible that morality can effect this happy coincidence of individual and collective interest, but I am not saying it does. Rather, I am saying that there just happens to be a certain degree of coincidence between individual and collective interest in a wide variety of situations. Further, such coincidence as there is happens to be a very good thing. The extent to which people act in the collective interest is far greater because of it. Thus, we would not expect a fundamental moral norm to shatter this coincidence; it would be inimical to cooperation if it did. If adhering to nonstrategic altruism would give others the opportunity and the incentive to free ride, whereas adherence to reciprocity would give others an incentive also to follow the norm, with the upshot of mutual adherence being the emergence of a pattern of cooperation, then reciprocity is the more plausible candidate for the status of fundamental norm governing cooperative relationships.

Against this, some would point to the fact that we decide individually whether to be moral and would infer that morality is a

Prisoner's Dilemma. In other words, we would all be better off if we all chose to be moral, but each individual's dominant strategy is to be immoral. By definition, then, our best strategy is to be immoral regardless of what other agents do. So, the argument concludes, other agents choosing to be moral cannot induce us to adhere to moral norms in the way I am supposing.

I reject this argument. Of course, we sometimes find ourselves in Prisoner's Dilemmas, but I deny that choosing to be moral is what makes them such. Imagine that Jane is trying to start up a grocery store. I am trying to buy some groceries, for I have finally found someone who pays cash for fence posts. In the first scenario, I find that grocery shopping consists of deciding whether to give Jane my money, hoping in either case that Jane will give me food. Likewise, Jane finds that being my grocer involves deciding whether to give me food, hoping in either case that I will give her money. The supposition that we must choose between defection and *nonstrategic altruism* makes this case a Prisoner's Dilemma. No matter what I decide, Jane is better off keeping her food; no matter what she decides, I am better off keeping my money. Noncooperation is a dominant strategy (see Figure 7.1).

In the second scenario, Jane and I can choose between defection and *reciprocation*. Thus, we are in the situation depicted by Figure 7.2. Jane chooses to offer groceries for money at a given rate. I choose whether to accept those offers. If Jane prefers $, a bundle of money, to *g*, a bundle of groceries, and I prefer *g* to $, then cooperation (i.e., exchanging *g* for $) is a dominant strategy. To suppose that morality asks us to be nonstrategic altruists, i.e., to put ourselves in the Prisoner's Dilemma of Figure 7.1 even when being a reciprocator is a viable option, amounts to supposing that morality is inimical to cooperation in general and to grocery stores in particular.

Figure 7.1
Trying to Get Groceries When Reciprocity Is Ruled Out

		Jane gives *g*	
		NO	YES
I give $	NO	*g* $	0 $ + *g*
	YES	*g* + $ 0	$ *g*

Figure 7.2
What Grocery Shopping Looks Like to Reciprocators

		Jane offers *g* for $	
		NO	YES
I offer $ for *g*	NO	*g* $	*g* $
	YES	*g* $	$ *g*

The moral strategy, then, is not merely a nice strategy but also the nice strategy that lets one use opportunities, when they arise, to give others an incentive to be nice, too—by acting so that the rewards produced by being nice are restricted to those who are being nice. Reciprocity dominates nonstrategic altruism, for it pays off at least as well and sometimes better from the individual point of view. Moreover, because it tends to induce more cooperation than does nonstrategic altruism, it tends to produce better results from the collective point of view as well.[4]

On the other hand, reciprocity does not dominate nonstrategic egoism, for it produces a lower individual payoff than free riding does in cases where others are cooperating nonstrategically and also in cases where you can free ride on reciprocators without being caught. But this is unimportant, for the point is not that reciprocal norms perfectly control the extent to which the positive externalities of cooperation spill over into the hands of noncooperators. The point is that they control it as well as it can be controlled by norms at all. In contrast, if nonstrategic altruism was the observed norm, you could free ride with impunity—genuine nonstrategic altruists would continue to supply you with a free ride even after they caught you.

Whether a purported moral norm promotes cooperation depends on whether it fosters the internalization of externalities. Unlike its rivals, reciprocity does foster the internalization process. Hence, it is superior to its rivals along a very important dimension. Nevertheless, the superiority of reciprocity and indeed its very meaning are clearer in two-person games than in many-person games. The next section considers the extent to which this superiority holds up when we switch to many-person games.

Before we proceed, however, we should stress that the point of our inquiry is to identify prerogative defeaters pertaining to a specific context: a public goods problem facing those who have the means to help solve it. Accordingly, my conclusions apply only to those for whom contributing is a real option. If a person needs a free ride to survive, for example, it would be harsh to say that morality requires the person to reciprocate. I have concluded that reciprocity ought to govern Jane's dealings with me, but I am not claiming that reciprocity ought to govern Jane's dealings with her infant son or with her blamelessly destitute neighbor. In other words, although society in the broadest sense is more than "a cooperative venture for mutual advantage," there are nevertheless many relationships—sub-societies, if you will—that genuinely do fit the Rawlsian description of cooperative ventures for mutual advantage. This discussion pertains only to those relationships, but it does not assume away the rest of society. Our conclusions apply only to agents who are self-sufficient in the sense that they do not need free rides from each other, but our argument does not unrealistically assume that all agents are self-sufficient in this sense, or that self-sufficient agents have always been self-sufficient, or that an agent who is self-sufficient in one context is necessarily self-sufficient in all others. Moreover, this discussion neither expresses nor implies an atomistic view of human nature; in other words, to say some people are self-sufficient in the sense described is not to deny that they are products of their cultures.

Reciprocity and Obligations to Cooperate

We can extend the preceding conclusion about reciprocity to many-person games in which consumption of the collective good at stake is exclusive. To wit, if we are allowed to play the game as reciprocators, we can deprive those who are not nice of the opportunity to consume the good until they change their strategy to something nicer. We must, however, be very cautious in extending this lesson to many-person games with goods the consumption of which is nonexclusive. Moreover, before we even begin to discuss whether reciprocity is coincident with both individual and collective interest in the many-person dilemma, we must first explain exactly what reciprocity means in the many-person context. This turns out to be an interesting puzzle.

In particular, what does reciprocity require of us when, if we cooperate with some people, we automatically create opportunities for *others* to free ride? Is it possible that I too am permitted to free ride in such a situation? If I am not permitted to free ride, then what? Do I have to act in a way that creates opportunities for others to free ride on me? What does reciprocity require when some are contributing a lot and others are free riding?

Does reciprocity in many-person dilemmas permit free riding merely because some others are free riding? I would say not. Nor would I say it requires one to contribute large amounts merely because a few others are. In fact, it does not identify any particular individual as the right one to respond to. Indeed, if I look for individuals to respond to, I miss the point. It is the group as a whole to which reciprocity demands my response. The benefit I receive is provided by the group as a whole, and funding for the project also comes from the group as a whole. What morality requires is that I reciprocate with the group as a whole. If I know what total benefits and total costs are and what my own benefits would be for any given contribution I might make, then being a reciprocator involves attempting to match my share of the total cost to my share of the total benefit.[5] This is what I take reciprocity to mean in many-person games.

As with any decision rule, of course, the less I know, the less useful will be the instruction to practice this version of reciprocity. I may not know what the total level of the good's provision will be, what total willingness to pay will be, or even what my own willingness to pay is. Uncertainty is even more likely when contributions involve effort and risk-sharing rather than straightforwardly measurable amounts of money. We could sometimes compensate for our uncertainty about what counts as reciprocation according to one standard by shifting to a slightly different standard. In some cases—telethons come to mind—we have fairly precise information about total contributions but know very little about total benefits. The reasonable response in such cases would be to treat total contributions as the relevant baseline for computing our own shares, for that is the only possible baseline that gives us sufficient information to act as reciprocators. (Even so, I would say that total contribution is not fundamental—when we know that our own benefit is out of proportion to that of others, it seems to me we ought to adjust our own contribution accordingly.)[6]

Why might practicing this sort of reciprocity be the best an agent can do in a telethon situation? Suppose you treat the rest of the group as the "partner" with whom you are supposed to reciprocate. By taking total contributions into account, you implicitly take everyone's contribution into account. Likewise, for every dollar you contribute, the total contribution to which other reciprocators respond is thereby larger by one dollar. This means that the presence of reciprocators gives you greater incentive to contribute more, because if they are committed to contributing in proportion to their benefit (or in proportion to total contributions, for that matter) and if your contribution increases their benefit (or increases total contributions), then you can lever reciprocators' contributions upward by increasing your own. The most dramatic example of people acting on this principle is the phenomenon of matching grants, i.e., large donations offered on the condition that the sum be matched by contributions from other sources. By presenting himself as a reciprocator, the large donor gives others an incentive to contribute more.

Moreover, the more people who contribute as reciprocators, the more profitable it becomes to contribute as a reciprocator yourself. If you would rather that everyone contribute a dollar than that no one does, then in the limiting case where everyone else is willing to reciprocate by contributing a dollar if you do, it becomes rational (i.e., a Nash equilibrium strategy) for you to contribute your share.

Admittedly, this is not exactly how reciprocity works. In fact, in a group of n reciprocators (Jane and $n - 1$ others), the others respond to Jane's contribution of c not by contributing c but rather by contributing their share, that is, $1/n$th, of the resulting rise in total contributions. In other words, they contribute c/n, a relatively trivial amount if n is large. But they also respond in turn to each other's contributions, so total contributions will gradually rise as these secondary responses work themselves out. Will Jane's contribution of c eventually elicit a group response of $(n - 1)c$, or will it elicit something considerably less, perhaps so much less that it is not rational for Jane to contribute for the sake of eliciting that response?

The proof that these incremental responses do eventually sum to $(n - 1)c$ is as follows: If Jane contributes c, each of the $n - 1$ reciprocators initially responds by contributing c/n. This new influx of $(n - 1)c/n$ in turn elicits a further response from each of the $n - 1$ reciprocators, and so on. Following is the equation giving the group response of the $n - 1$ reciprocators to Jane's contribution of c:

$$\text{Group response} = (n\text{-}1)[c/n + ((n\text{-}1)/n)(c/n) + ((n\text{-}1)/n)^2\,(c/n) + \ldots]$$

The formula within the square brackets gives each reciprocator's individual response. These individual responses are sums of the initial response plus an infinite series of echoes (with each echo equivalent to $1/n$th of the previous response) multiplied by $n - 1$ because there are a total of $n - 1$ previous responses to which each reciprocator responds.[7] We now manipulate this equation as follows:

$$=(n-1)c\ [1/n + ((n-1)/n)(1/n) + ((n-1)/n)^2\ (1/n) + ...]$$
$$=(n-1)c\ (1/n + 1/n\ [(n-1)/n + ((n-1)/n)^2 + ...]$$

The series within the square brackets sums to $n - 1$, according to the formula for obtaining sums of converging infinite series. (See any first-year college algebra text; I used Brixey and Andree, 1954, p. 189.) Thus we can substitute to obtain

$$=(n-1)c\ (1/n + 1/n[n-1])$$
$$=(n-1)c\ (1/n + (n-1)/n)$$
$$=(n-1)c\ (n/n)$$
$$=(n-1)c$$

So the amount contributed by the group of $n - 1$ reciprocators in response to Jane's contribution of c does sum to $(n - 1)c$. And by hypothesis, when everyone contributes c, this produces a return R sufficient to make everyone better off, including Jane, the original contributor. Therefore, it was rational for Jane to contribute c and thereby set in motion the series of contributions that resulted in her receiving R.

Of course, this is a pure and limiting case. The proof reveals something about the logic of reciprocity, but it is not meant to be realistic. What happens if we give up the unrealistic assumption that everyone else in the group is a reciprocator? To generalize from the limiting case, suppose that m individuals in the group are reciprocators and that there is some amount Jane could contribute such that reciprocators would each respond by contributing c. (The smaller m is, the larger her contribution must be to bring this about.) That is, each reciprocator's response would eventually add up to c, after they responded in turn to each other's responses to Jane. Because each of the m contributions of c produces a marginal return of r to each individual, this means Jane's contribution yields her an indirect return of *mr*, in addition to the marginal return generated directly by her contribution. Contributing this sum will be a Nash equilibrium strategy whenever *mr* added to the marginal return of her contribution exceeds the cost. And in any event, *mr* plus her direct marginal return is the gain Jane forgoes if she does not contribute. Hence, free riding will still be possible, but it will not be free, and the more reciprocators there are (i.e., the larger *m* is), the more expensive it will be.[8]

The injunction to be a reciprocator does not track self-interest nearly as well in the many-person dilemma as it does in Axelrod's two-person dilemmas (discussed earlier in this chapter), but it tracks self-interest better than one might have thought possible. The notion of reciprocity formulated here for the many-person dilemma gives others a certain incentive to remain or become reciprocators. Moreover, reciprocators also contribute their share of the cost of the public goods projects undertaken by their group. Jane's decision to be a reciprocator does not guarantee (and may not even greatly affect the probability of) public goods production. But for the moment, we are not talking about what a society can do to guarantee public goods provision; we are talking about what individuals can do when faced with the choice of how much to contribute. The process of internalizing externalities by adopting reciprocal norms in many-person dilemmas obviously cannot be a complete success, but again, the point is that, all other things equal, moral norms are those norms that succeed as well as norms can. The superior norm along this dimension has, by that very token, the better claim to being a moral norm.

Therefore, I conclude that in the context of voluntary public goods production, reciprocity is the pertinent moral principle. This principle normally is part of the foundation of the prerogative not to cooperate with others, for it allows one to cooperate with others on condition that they cooperate in return. Reciprocity, however, also grounds the prerogative defeater. It identifies the point at which prerogatives are defeated as the point at which exercising the prerogative not to cooperate becomes tantamount to free riding. Thus, it is reciprocity rather than considerations of utility that directly underlies the prerogative defeater associated with individual cost-benefit gaps. When faced with public goods problems, one should, to the best of one's knowledge and ability, pay a proportion of the total cost that is equal to one's proportion of the total benefit. (One might contribute in the expectation that total contributions will eventually rise to match one's own. This too is a form of reciprocity. Or one might go beyond reciprocity, contributing more than one expects ever to be matched by the contributions of others. Going beyond reciprocity is one's prerogative but, in this context, not one's duty. And if other people find themselves able to count on one to contribute large amounts whether or not they contribute, one's large contributions may come to be doing more harm than good.) Being a reciprocator is the best one can unilaterally do to bring about collective action at levels satisfactory to oneself and others. When morality tells an agent to do this, it has done everything it can[9]—unless it goes so far as to permit the agent to *force* others to contribute, which brings us to the topic of restriction defeaters.

A Foundation for Moral Norms

I argued that reciprocity is superior to its rivals as a norm for governing self-sufficient individuals in situations offering the possibility of cooperation for mutual advantage. I then used this conclusion to explicate prerogative defeaters, in the process answering the question of when we are obligated to help produce public goods. The question of when others may force us to help produce public goods is another and even more difficult question. To answer it, we must make further commitments, at deeper levels, to substantive moral theory.

What might such a theory look like? Because we have already drawn conclusions about the status of reciprocity as a moral norm and about the existence of both prerogatives and their defeaters, a theory would do well to support these conclusions. We must also be able to use the theory to draw conclusions about when we may be forced to produce public goods, for that is the point of devising the theory.

Obviously, these tests are by no means the only tests a theory of morals should pass. An exhaustive defense of the theory I outline here would require a book in itself. Indeed, since I have not written such a book, I cannot be certain that an exhaustive defense of the theory is possible. Yet despite the risk involved in venturing into this area, I think it is important to give at least an example of how my analysis of rights and defeaters, when combined with a substantive moral theory, can yield answers to the question of when others are permitted to force us to help produce public goods. And so I offer the theory in that spirit. I first state the theory, touching on its implications for reciprocal norms, and then turn to the question of when restrictions are defeated.

I have assumed that morality is not inimical to cooperation. Consider the following question as a foundational test of purported moral norms. "Would this norm be conducive to society's success?" A question that immediately comes to mind is, conducive to society's success *if what*? Under what conditions? So let us be more specific. "Would this norm be conducive to society's success if everyone adhered to it?" This sounds rather consequentialist, and also rather plausible. John Harsanyi, to give one recent example, has defended a theory of this kind.[10]

But it is not quite right. To suppose that everyone adheres to a norm is to abstract from the question of how people actually respond to it. This abstraction is a mistake, for whether a norm is conducive to a society's success turns directly on the question of how people in that society actually respond to it. An alternative test of purported moral norms is the question, "Is this norm conducive to a cooperative society's success, given how people will react both to it and to agents guided by it?" A complicated question, to be sure. Yet I think this is the question we ultimately ask (and are right to ask) when we subject a norm to moral assessment. For the sake of putting a name on this foundation and test of moral norms, I shall dub it the *feedback theory* of morality.

One might wonder why a cooperative society should be considered a moral ideal. To answer this, consider what a cooperative society is and what the alternatives to it are. That individuals make their own decisions and pursue their own plans has a bearing on what can count as a cooperative society. Most people have plans of some sort, and one can safely assume that other individuals typically are more or less intent on pursuing their own, notwithstanding the fact that personal projects are shaped and rendered meaningful to some degree by interactions with others and typically are motivated in part by a desire to contribute to society.

What makes a society cooperative, then, is the extent to which its members have the opportunity to develop and pursue their plans in peace and to interact in mutually helpful ways. (People may participate in organizations—e.g., governments, firms, communes, families—but they still have their own plans, notwithstanding that bringing those plans to fruition involves relying on and perhaps taking direction from other people.) As an alternative ideal, a noncooperative society would be one in which people do not have the opportunity to pursue their plans, or do not pursue them in peace, or do not interact in mutually helpful ways, or perhaps do not develop plans at all. Thus, we do not need to formulate feedback theory in terms of *cooperative* society, but I think feedback theory's endorsement of this ideal is reasonable. Moreover, this explicit endorsement makes feedback theory more obviously relevant to the public goods questions that led me to formulate it.

It is also worth saying a bit more here about what it means for society to succeed. Success, of course, is not a precise concept, and there is an advantage here in not trying to make it precise. We could say that society as a cooperative venture is successful if it maximally (or sufficiently) satisfies preferences. In contrast, we could interpret success in terms of conduciveness to happiness (i.e., what is good for people as opposed to what people want). We could adopt a eudaimonist conception of human flourishing or a Kantian conception of autonomy as that which a successful society promotes. Or we could employ various conceptions of society's health as an organic whole. The advantage of not making a commitment to any one of these is that they all point to the same result: Moral norms *reconcile* individual interests rather than *repudiate* them. Reconciling individual interests with each other—by allowing people pursuing their own plans to internalize positive externalities where possible, for example—also reconciles individual interests as well as possible (albeit imperfectly) with collective interest. Effecting this reconciliation is conducive to society's success as a cooperative venture by any of the standards of success just mentioned.[11]

Feedback theory does not ask what norms would be conducive to cooperation if everyone followed them. Nor does it ask what norms would be conducive to cooperation if one follows them but others do not. In the real world, other people's behavior is a variable, a variable that one's own behavior can sometimes influence. Thus, for a given norm, we must ask: (1) Will people who follow it give each other the incentive to keep it up? (2) Will people who follow it give people who are not following it an incentive to start? (3) Will the pattern that emerges promote cooperation? These are the conditions by which the real world determines whether or not a norm is conducive to cooperation.[12]

Nonstrategic altruism is, on its face, conducive to cooperation. Reciprocity is, on its face, conducive to cooperation in the same way. We see the difference between the two norms when we consider the reaction their adherents tend to get from other agents: Reciprocity induces others to reciprocate; nonstrategic altruism induces others to free ride. Insofar as agents can choose which of these two norms to follow, morality, according to feedback theory, counsels the choice of reciprocity. Reciprocity is conducive to successful cooperation because reciprocators give each other an incentive to keep it up. Further, they give people who do not reciprocate an incentive to start. And as reciprocity thus weaves itself into the social fabric, that society will become one that promotes cooperation, and by promoting cooperation, it will flourish.

Although morality permits and requires reciprocity in cooperative endeavors, there is no presumption here that it requires or even permits reciprocity in other areas of interpersonal action. (For instance, morality might not permit reciprocity in the imposition of harms.) There is no telling what strategies might be available or what moral norms might be salient in situations where internalizing externalities is not the issue. Thus, which norms feedback theory picks out as governing other contexts is an open question. In particular, with people who are incapable of reciprocation, that choice disappears as an option, and either nonstrategic altruism or some other strategy altogether may rise to the fore.

Feedback theory is an attempt to address both the fundamental independence of people as decisionmakers and the fundamental interdependence of people as bearers of the consequences of individual decisions. As an individual, what I should do is, as a matter of course, inextricably bound up with what we should do, and this fact makes morality what it is. Morality's answer to "What should I do?" fosters individual actions the upshot of which is the kind of de facto answer to "What should *we* do?" that allows people to flourish within the context of their patterns of mutual dependence.

Feedback theory presumably has shortcomings, as do other more general theories of morality. Moreover, its implication that morality incorporates reciprocal norms is not particularly novel. (This is as it should be, of course. We would not believe a theory that yielded principles we had never heard of.) But the reason feedback theory gives for why reciprocal norms are the fundamental moral norms of cooperation is, I think, the real reason. It is not that being a reciprocator maximizes utility, and it is not that reciprocity can be universalized. The real reason concerns the feedback that reciprocity gives to cooperators. Reciprocity is the backbone of a cooperative society's morality for the simple reason that reciprocity is the backbone of cooperation.

On Being Forced to Cooperate

Choosing whether to enter into cooperative endeavors is normally our prerogative. Ordinarily, this prerogative facilitates the practice of reciprocity and the consequent internalization of externalities and is thereby conducive to society's success as a cooperative venture.[13] But when others are helping to produce public goods that we value, allowing us not to cooperate is tantamount to allowing us to free ride. Our prerogative is thus defeated, with the result that cooperating becomes obligatory. With prerogative defeaters, the question of legal norms does not arise; prerogatives concern what an agent can and cannot do with her own property.[14] Their defeat does not remove the restriction against seizing her property. Restrictions, on the other hand, concern what *others* can and cannot do with her property, so the question of when they are defeated determines the possible scope of justified legal interference.

We discussed egoism, altruism, and reciprocity as modes of interaction among rational agents. This list of strategies presumes that interaction is voluntary. Once we consider using force, we have to step back, for we really are considering a fourth kind of strategy.

The restrictions implicit in property rights apply even to those who have the power to force other people to cooperate. Thus, they limit what states can take from people for the sake of public goods production. Yet the teleological rationale for restrictions is that they promote cooperative society (by internalizing externalities, thereby discouraging free riders). Therefore, the rationale for restrictions is self-limiting, because it would be inconsistent with that rationale for restrictions to prohibit the performance of actions that a cooperative society requires.

Coercive public goods provision might sometimes be a case in point. When a society can survive if and only if a certain public good is coercively produced, even the most rigorous reading of the restriction's self-limits must allow that the cost-gap summation associated with producing the good is large enough to defeat restrictions.

The most rigorous reading is also the most appropriate one. When we create mechanisms for coercively internalizing externalities, we simultaneously create mechanisms for generating externalities, for those who gain control of coercive fundraising mechanisms simultaneously gain the power to decide how much to spend on their projects without having to pay the costs of their decisions. (They can prevent free riding by forcing everyone to help produce public goods that everyone wants, but they also can facilitate free riding by forcing everyone to help produce so-called public goods that in fact benefit only a chosen few.) Creating such mechanisms for the purpose of *internalizing* externalities therefore makes sense only in desperate circumstances. Once the crisis is over—even supposing the coercive mechanism has effectively internalized externalities and thereby solved the immediate public goods problem—there is now yet another coercive mechanism in the world, waiting to fall into the wrong hands.

Be that as it may, suppose there are cases in which coercion is necessary to help produce certain public goods in amounts needed to preserve a cooperative society; voluntary efforts alone are insufficient to sustain the society. For example, citizens of a certain country long at peace may come to forget that an unobtrusive but still expensive level of military preparedness is, under their particular circumstances, a precondition of maintaining the peace along their own borders. They begin to divert their funds to other projects, both private and public, whenever they have a choice and thus defense funding declines toward a level at which their borders will no longer be secure. Only some form of coercive taxation will prevent defense funding from dropping below that level. Add to this story the supposition that the coercive power unleashed to help secure the state's borders will not itself be the society's undoing (if and when it falls into the hands of nonaltruists). According to feedback theory, the restriction against forcing citizens to help provide for their own defense is defeated in such a case.[15]

Conclusion

We have analyzed property rights and their defeaters and have given an example of how we might devise a moral theory to give normative content to this analysis for the purpose of identifying the points at which restriction defeaters are actually triggered. We also considered an argument that reciprocity is a moral norm and that it gives us an answer to the question of when prerogative defeaters are triggered. The concept of reciprocity is most readily applied to the production and exchange of private goods, but also has striking applications to the production of public goods. These results constitute my attempt to determine when we are obligated to help produce public goods and when others are permitted to force us to help.

Had we a sufficiently precise characterization of cooperative society and of what it means to say that a cooperative society can survive if and only if it coercively solves a public goods problem, the point at which restrictions were defeated would (according to feedback theory) become an empirical matter. Likewise, feedback theory implies that the point at which prerogatives are defeated is an empirical matter, notwithstanding the difficulty involved in acquiring the relevant data on total benefits, total contributions, and so on.

Perhaps we face or will face public goods problems that are so recalcitrant and so catastrophic that we will ultimately perish from inability to afford either coercive or voluntary solutions. Still, I think we must explore what we realistically can expect from voluntary efforts in particular cases. Laboratory studies such as those discussed in Chapter 6 and field data from both historical and contemporary sources can give us an idea of how pressing the need is for alternative means of providing particular public goods in particular cases. We also need to know how to use coercive means of providing public goods in a sufficiently delicate way that the result supplements the voluntary effort rather than obliterates it.

Chapters 2 and 3 together argued that particular applications of the public goods argument provide a teleological grounding of principles that in turn serve to emergently justify the institution of enforced property rights. Added to the present chapter's argument that the institution of property is teleologically justified, this implies that at least a minimal form of the state is (in both senses) justified. The moral framework deployed in this chapter, however, also reveals the general limits of the public goods argument's usefulness. The restriction against coercion inherent in property rights owes its rationale to its role in promoting a cooperative society—the kind of society in which people can develop and pursue their own plans in peace. When coercive production is necessary for the survival of such a society, then the rationale for the restriction against coercion in that case is undermined. On the other hand, when coercive public goods production is not necessary for such a society's survival—i.e., if people would be able to develop and pursue their own plans in peace without coercion—then the restriction against coercion remains very much in force. And given that coercion itself undermines people's ability to develop and pursue their own plans in peace, it makes good sense that public goods problems defeat the restriction only when coercive production of public goods is necessary for a cooperative society's survival.

Therefore, concerning the nature and scope of state activity that can be justified specifically by the public goods argument, the state would be limited to helping society provide those public goods without which cooperative society cannot survive—those institutions for keeping the peace and resolving disputes that characterize the minimal state, plus those public goods that involve overcoming what would otherwise be catastrophic negative externalities. This list would also include those public goods, if any, without which children would never grow up to become the more or less self-sufficient moral agents whose existence is presumed both by the public goods argument and by my moral framework for evaluating that argument. Some subtractions from this list might also prove to be in order, for the fact that a good is needed does not entail that coercion is needed to produce it. The public goods argument justifies creating only such coercive mechanisms as are worth the threat to society that their existence implies, given the alternative goods (both public and private) that would otherwise be produced voluntarily. The public goods argument by itself can justify more than a minimal state, perhaps, but not a great deal more. The justification of big government requires a different kind of argument.

Appendix: Rawls on Justice

John Rawls says a society is *well-ordered* when it advances the good of its members and is regulated by a public conception of justice (Rawls, 1971, p. 5). Chapter 7 discussed how reciprocity helps secure one defining feature of a well-ordered society: its tendency to advance the good of its members. Consider Rawls's second requirement. It was Plato's opinion that the just person cannot operate so as to encourage others to be more unjust (*Republic*, section 335). This has to be right, at least as a general rule. Accordingly, justice would not ordinarily require nonstrategic altruism; if it did, the just person would have to operate in a way that induces others to free ride. And if justice requires nonstrategic altruism, free riding ipso facto qualifies as unjust. Ergo, justice would be encouraging injustice. Hence, justice does not require nonstrategic altruism.

Whatever justice is, that just action typically will not encourage others to be more unjust means that what justice requires will track the discussion of this book on internalizing externalities and thereby reducing the scope for free riding. Justice mandates reciprocity, at least in dealings between those who are capable of reciprocation.

Although there is not much more that can be said here about justice without going well beyond the scope of this book, let me remark that, nowadays, justice is often thought of as specifying how to distribute a society's cooperative surplus. According to Rawls, original contractors choose "principles which are to assign basic rights and duties and to determine the division of social benefits" (Rawls, p. 11). Principles of *entitlement*, which ascribe rights to people, are what Rawls is talking about. They are, I admit, the kind of thing that original contractors would pick. Unlike me, however, Rawls believes this amounts to choosing principles of justice. The principles of justice "are the object of the original agreement. They are the principles that free and rational persons concerned to further their own interests would accept in an initial position of equality as defining the terms of their association" (Rawls, p. 11).

But surely whether such choices accord with justice is a contingent matter. Even behind what Rawls calls the veil of ignorance (Rawls, p. 136ff), contractors remain quite capable of picking rules of entitlement that would offend our sense of justice. Perhaps the veil deprives them of the knowledge they would need to do so profitably. Nevertheless, although the veil arguably makes doing so irrational, they are still capable of it. This would not be so if their choices were principles of justice by definition. Of course, Rawls could say that only their *rational* choices are principles of justice by definition, but then that draws attention to the oddness of supposing that it is rational to choose in accordance with a "maximin" rule. Consider that individuals who really used maximin would necessarily choose a difference principle that ranged over individuals rather than over class representatives. This is not a particularly original observation. It can be found, for example, in Nozick (1974, p. 190). But it makes me wonder why Rawls stops short of maximin's logical conclusion.

The fact is that the maximin decision procedure was merely Rawls's vehicle. It did not choose his destination for him. Rawls already knew where he wanted to go and maximin (conjoined to his specification of the original position) took him there. The fact that it does not stop quite where he wanted to get off suggests that no other decision procedure stops as close. That Rawls wanted a particular result, rather than just taking the decision procedure where it led him, suggests that he knows justice is not the outcome of the contract. It is an antecedent constraint on the contract (and the nature of that constraint is not the kind of thing rational bargainers get to *pick*). Rawls wants the outcome to accord with (be in reflective equilibrium with) that antecedent constraint. Even supposing that a society's entitlement system can be reconstructed as the outcome of a social contract, it remains the case that justice already has a formal nature prior to the emergence of an entitlement system.

On the other hand, there is a difference between public conceptions of justice and justice per se. Although justice per se is prior to any particular institutional arrangement, public conceptions of justice are another matter. Conceptions of what is just are, I would say, largely driven by *epistemically justified expectations.* These consist of expectations generated by induction from experience about how other people in similar situations have been treated. Epistemically justified expectations are, to a significant degree, generated by the institutions themselves.

But public conceptions of justice are only institution-driven to a degree. The principle that people are due the fruits of their labor is, I suspect, a feature of public conceptions of justice that transcends institutional input. (I believe this principle is also part of justice per se, but the following remarks are meant as a descriptive account of its public conception, not as a normative account of the nature of justice per se.) What makes this principle especially interesting, however, is that what people are due is a function of what they do with what they have, and what they have is in part determined by legislators. So the content of what people are due (i.e., the actual bundles they have coming to them) is partly institution-driven after all. Thus, legislators cannot aim for a "just" allocation of bundles when devising institutions; what a "just" allocation amounts to (in the public conception) is determined only after institutions are in place. (Think of it this way: You can steer toward an automobile, but not if it is the one you are driving.)

Nevertheless, people are (or will be publicly conceived of as being) due the fruits of their labors whether or not institutions play a role in determining what those fruits are. In other words, the particular content of what people are due is partly institution-driven, but the general form (i.e., the general idea that people are, after all, due the fruits of their labors) is not. The form can serve as a constraint on the devising of institutions, even if the content cannot serve as a goal.

Notes

Chapter 1

1. Howard Margolis claims, "It is not too strong a statement to say that societies, and hence politics, exist because public goods exist" (1982, p. 9). I take Margolis to mean that societies arise as responses to public goods problems. Whether or not his statement is too strong, it certainly illustrates the salience of the public goods argument in the social sciences.

2. Two thousand years earlier, Glaucon challenged Socrates (in Plato's *Republic*, sec. 359) to prove that being just is rational even if we suppose that the material rewards of being just accrue exclusively to the unjust. The challenge, in other words, is to show that when the material payoff of being just is a public good—enjoyed by everyone but its producers—there is nevertheless a hidden private benefit that makes it rational to produce this public good. As fascinating as Glaucon's challenge is, however, I think it was via Hobbes that the public goods argument began its rise to prominence in political philosophy.

3. This distinction does not, of course, exhaust logical space in the way that a less interesting division between teleological and non-teleological justification would. On the other hand, most and perhaps all of the historically important attempts at justification can be usefully classified as either emergent or teleological, although some attempts will fit the paradigm better than others. For instance, an argument that the state commands our loyalty because it was teleologically justified in the past is neither emergent nor teleological, but nor is it an argument that many would care to defend. In any event, I think there is much to be learned about a given argument by seeing how well it fits the emergent or

teleological molds. For example, see the discussion of hypothetical consent arguments in the next section of this chapter.

4. But see Chapters 2 and 3. Insofar as moral borders are grounded in teleological considerations, and insofar as teleological justification proceeds by way of a weighing of alternatives, the shape taken by moral borders depends on how that shape compares with available alternatives. As teleologically justified institutions emerge, they create new alternatives and thereby have the potential to relocate such moral borders as otherwise would have precluded their justified emergence. To show that an institution relocates borders rather than simply crosses them, however, one has to show exactly how the logic that locates borders in a certain place is affected by that institution's emergence.

Chapter 2

1. Chapter 3 uses an analogous argument to justify state assumption of the right to punish those who violate property rights. I analyze property rights as conjunctions of prerogatives (one may use what one owns as one pleases, within limits) and correlative restrictions (other people may not use what one owns without permission, though this restriction also has limits). This analysis will become more important in Chapter 7, where it becomes the basis for analyzing when society's need for public goods overrides property rights.

2. Geoffrey Miller (1987) and Loren Lomasky (1987, pp. 129ff) are exceptions. Their arguments are radically different from mine but consistent with it. David Gauthier (1986, p. 203), Robert Nozick (1974, p. 178n), and Carol Rose (1987, pp. 429ff) believe the system as a whole, as opposed to individual acts, can satisfy the Proviso.

3. A tragedy of the commons is a situation in which overusing common resources costs more than it is worth, from a collective viewpoint, but is individually rational because the overuser reaps all of the benefits of overuse, while others pay most of the cost.

In passing, Carol Rose (1987, p. 436) and John Sanders (1987, p. 381) mention the prospect of commons tragedies while arguing that property institutions are, after all, a good thing. More generally, we can follow Demsetz (1967) in taking property rights to be, in part, a response to externalities—the side effects of individual pursuits that spill over into the lives of others without their consent. Degrading the commons is a negative externality. The cost falls mainly on the group rather than on the individual or subgroup that creates the cost. Upgrading the commons is a positive externality. The benefit falls mainly on the group rather than on the individual or subgroup that creates the benefit. Converting the commons to parcels held by individuals or subgroups tends to internalize both kinds of externality. (To "internalize an externality" is to alter the situation so as to make the external cost or benefit bear more fully on the decisions of those who are generating it.) Historical records examined by Anderson and Hill (1975) suggest that property institutions evolve whenever implementing exclusion mechanisms (e.g., fences and livestock branding) becomes generally cost-effective.

My argument, however, is different. I use the logic of the commons to reconstruct the satisfaction conditions of the Lockean Proviso itself. Because the Proviso concerns what is just as well as what is good, reconstructing its satisfaction conditions goes beyond the subject of prudent social policy. The project also bears upon the nature of justice in acquisition. (Or we could say that my argument goes directly to the question of emergent justification, whereas Demsetz's argument bears only on teleological justification.)

4. He might, for instance, have it in mind that the emerging distribution of resources would never have been chosen by constitutional convention. The present chapter neither uses nor responds to contractarian arguments, but a good example of such an argument can be found in John Roemer (1989, p. 87). Likewise, this chapter neither uses nor responds to natural rights theories, although if particular rights-claims were inconsistent with the conclusions developed here, I would reject them for that reason.

5. A caveat is in order here: The Levelers (an English Puritan sect active in the early part of the 17th century) thought there is something wrong when people have to depend on others for things they need. Thus, taking his cue from the Levelers, Locke might have objected to the necessity of trade in land over generations and to the asymmetrical relations of dependence that could spring from it. (I thank John Simmons for suggesting this.) Then again, the more property that was preserved in useful condition, the less that buyers of it would be at the mercy of particular sellers. So the Levelers' objection cuts both ways, making it hard to know what Locke would have said about it in this context.

6. Making a related point, John Sanders remarks that people have thought it unfair that latecomers should be excluded from owning prop-

erty by the rules for initial acquisition of unowned resources. Indeed, he says (1987, p. 385): "That *would* be unfair. But [latecomers] are *not* excluded from acquiring property by these rules. They are, instead, excluded from being the first to own what has not been owned previously. Is *that* unfair?"

7. Many people have thought that we ought to be able to use the Proviso to criticize the sheer largeness of some holdings. At least under some extreme circumstances, however, this will not be true. For example, consider the problem of explaining why people should not be allowed to appropriate the entire stock of a vital natural resource, such as a region's only water hole. (See Nozick, 1974, p. 179.) The Proviso, according to my reading of it, offers no such explanation, at least not on its face. On the contrary, it could conceivably require such appropriation, if that is truly what it would take to preserve the water hole. It does not follow that any size of appropriation is justified, even in such extreme cases. What does follow, however, is that to criticize an appropriation on the grounds that it was too large, one would need to refer to applicable principles of justice other than to the Proviso.

Chapter 3

1. Nozick is concerned with showing that the DPA eventually evolves into an institution that both monopolizes the use of force and provides universal protection within its domain (1974, p. 23). Against Nozick, I consider neither of these features to be essential properties of the state. First, actual states do not offer universal protection. They do not even offer citizenship to everyone in their geographical domains. Nor would a state that permits the extradition of a person living peacefully in its domain, for crimes allegedly committed elsewhere, thereby cease to be a state. Second, many states do not even attempt to monopolize the use of force, and those that try do not succeed. Nor would a state that legalizes bounty hunting, say, thereby cease to be a state.

I expressed doubt in the Preface that states really have essential properties. At any rate, I suspect that statehood is best viewed as a matter of degree. But to the extent that states share an essence, I think a state is essentially a final authority in disputes, and one part of this final authority is the right to punish.

2. Another possible problem arises if the contractual obligations

hold only for a limited time. If so, then a client-citizen's obligations would be open to renegotiation from time to time. I thank Nat Sears for this observation.

3. This proposal is not intended to prejudice the issue of whether there are also other restrictions on the right to punish. Presumably there are. Nor does it presume any particular analysis of what punishment is; suffice it to say that we are not talking about self-defense, but we are talking about "judging one's own case" after the fact.

Nozick (1974, p. 88) also suggests that individuals have only the right to practice the least risky method of self-help. (I thank Roderick Long for reminding me of this, and in the process stimulating me to develop the theory presented in the text.) But Nozick is talking about the risk of punishing an innocent person or overpunishing a guilty one, not about the risk to innocent bystanders.

4. Moreover, Nozick's principle of compensation also becomes unnecessary because the independent's right to punish is not abrogated. Instead, it simply reaches its limits. Thus, no compensation is due. In Nozick's story, the principle of compensation is needed to morally constrain the DPA's incentive to wield its power overzealously. In my story, the moral constraint is built into the power itself. (The state acquires the right to punish *only* when it becomes the least risky vehicle for exercising this right.) If the DPA wields its power overzealously, it loses the moral right to wield it at all. (On the other hand, this does not entail that individuals will regain their right to self-help at the same time, because self-help might still be more risky than the unnecessarily risky methods of the state.)

5. Jules Coleman and Jody Kraus (1988, p. 32) make the point that liability rules can be thought of as protecting property rights only insofar as property rights are thought of as fundamentally protecting the agent's interests rather than the agent's autonomy: "In the classical liberal view, the right is the liberty, not the value (i.e., utility) to anyone of having or exercising that liberty.... Because utility is not autonomy, and because liability rules neither confer nor respect a domain of lawful control, liability rules cannot, on this view, protect rights."

6. For further reading, I recommend the essay "Imposing Risks" in Judith Jarvis Thomson (1986).

7. This is a hypothetical consent argument, of course. I address what I take to be the underlying teleological justification of the minimal state without doing too much violence to the contractarian motivation of the

original argument. For a more direct confrontation of Levin's contractarian project, see Christopher Morris (1988). For a well-taken response to an earlier version of my argument (Schmidtz, 1989) see Michael Levin (1989).

8. A technical analysis of Levin's argument might put it as follows. (The technical vocabulary is introduced in Chapter 4. Those not yet familiar with it can safely skip this note.) Levin supposes that the situation in which each of us is heavily armed and the situation in which each of us is lightly armed are both Nash equilibria. That is, we arm ourselves only because we fear each other. (If we were would-be aggressors, then we would have free rider problems as well as assurance problems and unilateral disarmament would only provoke attack. Thus, heavy armament would be the only equilibrium.) Suppose we are in the heavy armament equilibrium. If a government peacekeeper then interposes herself between us, she disturbs the equilibrium, for I can now make myself better off by unilaterally skimping a bit on my defense budget. You subsequently have two reasons to reduce your budget—not only is the government protecting you but I have now reduced my budget. So you now have reason to reduce your budget even more than I originally reduced mine. This triggers the downward spiral to the light armament equilibrium.

9. The idea makes a particularly interesting appearance in Loren Lomasky (1987, p. 70ff).

Chapter 4

1. Were the subject to arise, I would want self-defense to count as noncoercive, which is why I speak of the initiation of force rather than of the use of force.

2. Anthony de Jasay defines *jointness* as "the property of a good which enables one more person to use, consume or enjoy it, rely on, or otherwise benefit from it without the consumption, reliance, benefit, etc., of any other person being thereby reduced" (1989, p. 157). Most theorists take jointness or indivisibility to be synonymous with nonrivalry in consumption. But see Michael Taylor (1989, p. 7) for a distinction between not diminishing the *amount* of a good available for others (jointness) and not diminishing the *benefits* available for others (nonrivalry of consumption). De Jasay immediately infers from his own definition of

jointness: "If there can be a man-made good in truly joint supply, it is either available or not. The idea of making more of it available contradicts the idea of its jointness" (1989, p. 157). It is worth noting that I do not interpret nonrivalry (or jointness, for that matter) as having this implication. Instead, I would distinguish between making the good *more available* and making *more of the good* available. Suppose a kind of antimissile defense, say, is jointly supplied. It follows that such protection as exists cannot be made more available to the group than it already is, but there is no contradiction in supposing that we could make more of it available simply by adding more antimissile weapons to the existing stockpile. We might, in fact, be glad to have someone supply us with more. Likewise, nonrivalry does not exclude the possibility that providing more of the good would be beneficial.

Also, note how group size affects the relationship between nonrivalry in consumption and the diminishing marginal return of investment in public goods production. The marginal benefit to an individual of a given contribution can be affected by group size. It is not, however, affected by the increasing number of *consumers*; nonrivalry in consumption entails that adding more consumers makes no difference to any individual's enjoyment of the good. Yet the marginal benefit of a given contribution is affected by the increasing number of *contributors*, if returns to scale are diminishing. The discussion in the text avoids this complication by assuming that marginal returns are not affected by the scale of investment.

3. Amartya Sen defines the assurance problem differently. According to Sen's now-standard definition, two conditions generate the problem. First, given the choice between mutual defection and mutual cooperation, each individual prefers mutual cooperation. Second, in the special case where everyone else cooperates, the individual prefers to cooperate also. Otherwise, the preference is to defect (Sen, 1967). The advantages of straying from Sen's definition will shortly be apparent. I summarize them in note 6 of this chapter.

The concept of the assurance problem (as I define it) can be traced back at least as far as Hobbes's *Leviathan*. An exceptional modern discussion of the assurance problem and how it might be solved can be found in Brubaker (1975). Tyler Cowen describes Schmidtz (1987a) as "an extension of Brubaker's analysis" (Cowen, 1988, p. 8), which is not an unflattering description, considering the quality of Brubaker's piece.

The concept of the free rider problem can be traced back at least to Hume's *Treatise of Human Nature* and Rousseau's *Second Discourse*. The canonical interpretation of public goods problems as Prisoner's Dilemmas is Russell Hardin's (1982).

4. That one strategy is better than another *in every case*, however, does not entail that it is the better strategy. You are better off in every case if you choose the top half of the matrix (by testifying) rather than the bottom half. Yet, to follow up on a point made by Michael Resnick (1987, p. 10), suppose your choice affects which case you will be in. (Suppose you suspect that your partner's final answer was "I will do whatever my partner does.") If you prefer the lower right box to the upper left box in Figure 4.2, then which strategy is better depends on what kind of "right-left" influence you expect your decision to have. It might be better to pick the lower half of the array, despite the fact that picking the upper half is better in every case. This suggests that the playing of dominant strategies is not *itself* a dominant strategy. Alternatively, we might simply stipulate (as it seems Resnick would do, although his discussion is not explicitly about strategies at all) that the dominant strategy concept applies only when your choice has no right-left influence.

5. The more formal analysis employed by Michael Taylor (1987, p. 16), who follows Russell Hardin (1982), characterizes the nature of the dominant strategy in a Prisoner's Dilemma as follows: Suppose that in a group of size n, m other individuals are contributing c, and each contribution produces a benefit r for the individual. The individual receives mr/n if he does not contribute and receives $[(m + 1)r/n] - c$ if he does contribute. (In other words, he gains $r - c$, except that r is discounted to the extent that the size of n entails crowding in the consumption of the good.) If c is greater than r/n, then noncontribution is a dominant strategy.

This analysis of the Prisoner's Dilemma is perfectly correct and formally identical to mine (except that I ignore crowding effects). I consider my analysis (which immediately follows in the text) more useful, however, because it separates the incentives to withhold into two psychologically very distinct categories, depending on how large the individual expects m to be.

6. I have strayed from Sen's definition of the assurance problem (see note 3) because I believe rational players would characteristically be more concerned about the amount of money contributed by other players rather than about how many of them are contributing. My analysis can also, unlike Sen's, be reconciled with standard assumptions about individual economic behavior. My interpretation, for instance, reveals the assurance problem to be an integral part of the Prisoner's Dilemma. My interpreta-

tion allows for the possibility that agents have some special preference to contribute that manifests itself only when everyone else is contributing, but unlike Sen's interpretation, mine does not assume any such special preference.

My solution to the assurance problem does not, however, depend upon this change in emphasis. One could just as easily offer a contract asking for pledges that were enforceable only if all other individuals also made pledges. But as I said, I do not believe that this is really what people need to be assured of. A requirement of unanimity might, in some cases, be an effective response to the free rider problem, but that is another issue, to be discussed later in this chapter.

7. For the record, I think that such a contract would probably be enforceable under current law. First, a bilateral conditional contract would not require that an actual payment be made in order to be binding. For instance, citing *Swanson* v. *Priest*, 58 A.2d 207, 95 N.H. 64 (1948), Arthur Corbin says: "The seller offers his promise to transfer land or goods in return for a promise of payment by the buyer. It is the buyer's promise to pay that is the consideration for the seller's promise to transfer. But the buyer's promise to pay is not the price of the land or goods; the price is the amount to be paid. In this case there is a contract as soon as the buyer accepts by making his requested promise; the consideration has been given, though the price has not been paid" (1950, section 501, p. 478).

Nor would an assurance contract be unenforceable simply because one of its conditions was not under the complete control of either party, as long as the conditions were determinate. "Suppose that A delivered the goods in exchange for B's promise to pay $100 *if and when his ship comes in*. We still say that A has a right, even though there is one additional fact necessary to a societal remedy, and even though that fact may never occur" (Corbin, 1950, section 626, p. 581). "As soon as the offer is accepted and there is mutual assent to the terms proposed, we use the term 'contract' and we begin to talk about A's "right" to payment. This is true even though the money is not yet due and even though it may never become due" (Corbin, section 626, p. 581).

8. A person may also feel a moral obligation to contribute. This factor cannot be lumped in with fringe benefits. In fact, it cannot be represented in the matrix at all, because feelings of moral obligation are not interests. A typical maximization problem posits a utility function and a budget constraint within the bounds of which the maximum value of that

utility function is sought. To posit fringe benefits is to posit that group-interest is part of the utility function. To posit moral obligation is also to posit group-interest, perhaps, but as part of the constraint under which maximization occurs rather than as part of the thing to be maximized. Put less formally, I can act in your interest either because I believe I like you or because I believe I owe you something; the two beliefs are not the same. How to decide what we owe each other is the topic of Chapter 7.

9. The point that collective goods can generally be marketed as excludable goods has been made forcefully by Kenneth Goldin (1977). Anthony de Jasay (1989, pp. 127-134) makes the related point that the cost of exclusion is partly a function of institutional arrangements; the degree of exclusiveness is chosen along with the choice of institutional arrangements and largely on the basis of social and cultural rather than technical considerations.

10. Because one's ability to pay for a good can affect how much one is willing to pay for it, a question arises as to whether cost shares should be or can be partly determined by ability to pay. Vernon Smith (1980, p. 597) relates the following evidence concerning how experimental subjects in laboratory situations, as their initial endowment rises, contribute more both as a percentage of their initial endowment and also as a percentage of the actual value to them of the public good in question.

An examination of mean bids by subjects in three parameter classes provides some insight into the nature of subject deviations from the Lindahl optimum. Subjects in class I having an endowment of 8, and a theoretical Lindahl equilibrium (LE) bid of 4, bid on average very close to 4. However, class II subjects with an endowment of 10 and a theoretical LE bid of 2, have a mean bid of 4.86. These subjects much prefer the private good to the public good, but apparently because of their relatively large endowments tend to "overcontribute" to the public good. Similarly, class III subjects with an endowment of 5 and an LE bid of 4, tend to "undercontribute" with a mean bid of 2.63. Hence the "rich" give more and the "poor" give less than is predicted by the LE bids.

Although the possibility of disproportionate participation by the relatively wealthy is encouraging for voluntary mechanisms, it has ominous implications for representative governments with the power to coerce. It implies that the rich will have a relatively strong tendency to overcome whatever collective action problems they may have in forming coalitions. Therefore, the degree to which a representative government satisfies the ideal of open and easy access by constituents is the same degree to which it will fail to satisfy the ideal of *equal* access. This is so because the rich and poor are not equally likely to form coalitions for the purpose of lobbying government to further their respective interests. Thus, the actual distribution of burdens imposed by a coercive system may indeed be correlated to individual endowments, but the direction of the correlation might not be one that anyone would care to defend. Such hazards are considered at length in Chapter 5.

11. An interesting discussion of experimental data on the incentive properties of a unanimity requirement can be found in Vernon Smith (1977). He found that the requirement led to agreement on an optimal outcome in a majority of cases, but for purposes of drawing conclusions about the theory developed here, the experiments surveyed in Chapter 6 are more pertinent.

Chapter 5

1. Eric Mack (1986) notes the possibility of devising conditional contracts that would be valid only if those known to have positive valuations made contributions commensurate with those valuations. He also notes that the existence of honest holdouts undermines the claim that coercive provision amounts to a "particularly benign paternalism." Jean Hampton (1987, p. 271) and Earl Brubaker (1975, p. 156) echo this, also noting that goods not naturally produced in steps can arbitrarily be made "step goods" by the terms of the offer to produce them. Prospective patrons thereby have incentives to contribute that stem not only from the marginal benefit of their prospective contribution but also from the fact that their contribution makes it more likely that the initial step in production will be adequately financed in the first place. This ground is also covered in Schmidtz (1987a), but not as well.

2. I use the term 'optimal' here in a technical sense. A situation is *Pareto-optimal* (i.e., optimal in the technical sense) when there is no way to make any player better off without also making at least one other player worse off.

3. An excellent account of how the sense of moral responsibility might influence contributions to public goods projects can be found in Sugden (1984). Elster (1989, especially chap. 5) offers a more general account of how social norms might influence collective action.

4. So long as there is a consumer demand for contract enforcement,

it appears to be the sort of private good that the market is generally quick to supply. Still, as a practical matter, the need for contract enforcement is only one of many hurdles the private sector must jump to be able to market *public* goods. Competition among entrepreneurs, for example, could also create problems, because it might interfere with fundraising drives for any particular project. To offset this, a pooling arrangement could be allowed if subscribers agreed that their commitments could be sold to alternative providers. It would be in the interest of all parties (at least all parties desiring the public good) to permit the buyout of contracts by competing entrepreneurs. In this way we would avoid the wasted duplication of services and also avoid the canceling out of competing interests. If economies of scale supported natural monopolies (say, in providing the roadwork for a newly built suburban subdivision) then natural monopolies would emerge. If not, they would not emerge. It is important to note that natural monopolies emerging by assurance contract would be emerging *under contract*. Consumers would be protected in advance from monopolistic pricing. An interesting discussion of the regulation of so-called natural monopolies can be found in Demsetz (1968).

Using universally desired goods as the main attractions of package-deal assurance contracts might not work when competing entrepreneurs were able to offer a more attractive product by dispensing with the rest of the package and just offering the universally desired good. This would be the case when the universally desired good is the only part of the package in which people are strongly interested. However, if there is no strong interest in the remainder of the package, then the lack of interest indicates that the remainder is not worth what it would cost to provide it. Thus, another apparent disadvantage of administering assurance contracts through private rather than government channels turns out to be a particularly interesting advantage instead. That is, if there was any advantage to be gained by offering public goods in packages—there might be if prospective customers were solicited as communities, say, rather than as individuals—then competition would ensure that entrepreneurs whose packages featured undesired goods would, all other things being equal, lose out to entrepreneurs who deleted the undesired goods from their proposal.

5. For example, see Reinhard Selten (1978) or Luce and Raiffa (1957, pp. 97-102). An excellent recent critique of the "backward induction paradox" can be found in Pettit and Sugden (1989).

6. For further discussion of the strategic significance of reputation, see Robert Frank (1988, chap. 4) and Gauthier (1986, chap. 6). Frank and

Gauthier both argue that cooperation occurs because, by adopting a cooperative disposition, individuals become more attractive to other cooperators and hence have more opportunities to enter mutually beneficial relationships. Frank also discusses how cooperative dispositions might be developed and how others might detect them.

Chapter 6

1. John Roemer (1988) provides a particularly useful analysis of the concept of exploitation.

2. Moving to an equilibrium is *Pareto-superior* if the move makes at least one player better off and makes no players worse off. Moving to an equilibrium is *Pareto-inferior* if the move makes at least one person worse off and no one better off. When Pareto-inferior moves occur, it is usually via intermediate moves whose immediate effect—before other players retaliate—is to make the player who moved temporarily better off. For the record, a *Pareto-optimal* outcome is one with respect to which no Pareto-superior moves are possible; there is no move that would make a given player better off without making at least one other player worse off.

3. Events of recent weeks, as I write in February 1990, suggest that the Soviets may soon make huge cuts in conventional forces in Eastern Europe. One would not expect such a bold strategy, except for the fact that it is partly a response to internal political and economic problems. The Soviets also hope to encourage the advocates of Western European neutrality and to weaken the North Atlantic Treaty Organization. Be this as it may, the announced cuts give the United States the opportunity to consider making substantial cuts of its own.

4. A great deal has recently been written on the ethics of nuclear deterrence and nuclear disarmament. For further reading, I recommend James Child (1986) and Gregory Kavka (1987).

5. For more on the distinction between economic policy and economic theory, see Alvin Roth (1986) and Charles Plott (1982). My discussion is especially indebted to the latter.

Chapter 7

1. Samuel Scheffler's terms, and the concepts they refer to, are slightly different from mine. Moreover, Scheffler doubts whether "agent-centered restrictions" have a rationale at all. Nevertheless, his discussion (1982) inspires my characterization of property rights.

2. The conditions of the tournament were as follows: Games were between pairs of players in a round-robin tournament. Each player had two choices on each move: cooperate or defect. The payoffs were fixed and known. At each move, players have access to the history of the game up to that move. To avoid the end-game effects of a predetermined final period, there was a fixed probability of the game ending on the next move.

There are a variety of strategies that embody norms of reciprocity. Some are "nicer" than others; for instance, some might involve defecting only after one's partner has defected on consecutive moves. Axelrod and Dion (1988) discuss a variety of factors that influence which reciprocal strategies are individually optimal. For example, in a situation where it is possible to defect by accident, despite having the best intentions, then up to a point one is better off ignoring occasional defections. I argue in the text that reciprocal strategies best promote cooperation given that individuals decide for themselves what strategy to follow; if, however, there turned out to be some alternative that is superior to the various forms of reciprocity in this respect, then by that very token, the superior strategy is the strategy my theory would really endorse.

3. I owe this observation to Russell Hardin.

4. Exceptions can arise in cases where particularly heroic or touching acts of nonstrategic altruism inspire people to respond in kind instead of responding by free riding. It is also true that if one wants to be touching or inspiring to others—if one wants to do more than simply get them to pay for their groceries—then nonstrategic altruism may recommend itself to individual rationality as well. I thank Michael McPherson for suggesting this point.

5. If the possibility of overcontribution is troublesome in a particular case, one would let one's contribution be a function of total benefits up to but not exceeding those associated with an efficient production level. See Robert Sugden (1984) and Joel Guttman (1987) for different accounts of the nature of reciprocity and its significance for public goods production.

6. Moreover, in a population of reciprocators, a person whose marginal benefit is relatively large has an incentive to make a relatively

large contribution because the larger response that the person can elicit by contributing more is worth that much more to the person.

I would also say that we should adjust our contribution when our opportunity cost is out of proportion to that of others. For instance, when the alternative we forgo by contributing is buying next week's groceries, as opposed to attending an opera, we have a legitimate reason not to contribute even when the benefit of providing the public good is held constant.

7. Technically speaking, since respondents are responding to total contributions at each step, and trying to ensure that their own contributions add up to *1/n*th of the *total* at that point, their responses must include responses to their own previous contributions as well as to each other's. That is why each respondent responds to n - 1 previous responses rather than only n - 2.

8. In a real telethon, it is also true that reciprocators would not respond in this continuous fashion. Rather, they would respond in more discrete steps to increases in total contributions. Even so, evidence of reciprocity is not hard to find. For example, it is not unusual to hear of challenge grants. The fire department, say, might agree to contribute a thousand dollars if the police department pledges a similar amount. Behavior under laboratory conditions also tends to conform to this version of reciprocity. When subjects are aware of total contributions and of the number of subjects in their group, as they were in the experiments of Robert Dorsey (unpublished), many of them determine their own contributions by dividing total contributions (minus their own) by the number of subjects (minus themselves), updating their contributions as the former number changes.

9. That is, reciprocal norms have done what they can in terms of helping the individual decide how much to contribute. More generally, morality typically would not preclude applying pressure to others by campaigning, scolding, and so on, as further ways of trying to ensure the project's success.

10. Harsanyi (1985, p. 44) says "the very purpose of rule utilitarianism is to identify the moral code that would maximize expected utility if it became the accepted moral code of society...." By an accepted moral code, Harsanyi means (p. 44) one that is followed by all rational and morally motivated people.

11. A more difficult case involves an ethical egoist standard of the good. My theory allows for moral norms that preserve such coincidence

as exists between individual and collective interest, and this is certainly amenable to ethical egoism, for the egoist also approves of norms that are conducive to individual and collective interest. The problem arises because my theory allows what ethical egoism denies—namely, that because individual interest sometimes fails to track collective interest, it also sometimes fails to track morality.

12. Feedback theory is neutral with respect to the question of whether there is any place in morality for the promulgation of unattainable ideals. We may entertain an arguably unattainable ideal of universal cooperation, but any norms rationalized by this ideal presumably must be rationalized by virtue of being conducive to realizing the closest feasible and worthwhile approximation of this ideal.

13. Oddly, certain kinds of negative externalities should be permitted, even encouraged. Specifically, affecting another party's property by only changing its market value is permissible. Forbidding such external effects (sometimes called *pecuniary* externalities) would amount to making it illegal to enter a market in competition with incumbents, because doing so ordinarily forces incumbents either to cut prices or lose business. The upshot is that there is a limit to what can be privatized. No one can own markets as such. An incumbent's share of the market can be taken away by his competitors. No one has to ask his permission. Markets as such will remain in the commons.

14. If the cost-gap summation was very large (and positive), it might defeat an individual's prerogative not to contribute even if that individual's own gap was negative. Consider the public good of quickly erecting dikes in a community suddenly threatened by floods. In such a case, it seems reasonable to suppose that able-bodied members of the community have no prerogative not to volunteer; the cooperative society whose morality underlies their prerogatives is going to underlie a lake unless they volunteer.

15. I previously discussed the possibility of a second kind of restriction defeater. If Jane's own cost-benefit surplus is large enough and obvious enough, so that it is clear that noncontribution would be tantamount to free riding on her part, this might be thought to defeat the restriction against taking her property. This is how a "quasi-paternalistic" argument for state coercion might enter the public goods picture. Left to their own devices, the group will not produce the public good, so by forcing its members to contribute, the government does for the group what its members (including Jane) want done but cannot do for themselves.

However, it would typically be almost impossible to show that the conditions for invoking this defeater had been met. One would have to make sure that the individuals being coerced really have positive cost-benefit gaps. But in fact, what the government does for people might be something that some people would rather the government not do at all, and especially not with their money. A means of obtaining accurate information about individual preferences would be required before one could acquire the empirical grounds for invoking a restriction defeater based on assumptions about individual cost-benefit gaps. (Moreover, if people actually had accurate information about each other's preferences, coercion might not be necessary for public goods production, because few people would have the audacity to free ride when they and everyone else knew how much they wanted the good in question.) The gap summation defeater discussed in the text is the more relevant option.

References

Anderson, Terry L., and Hill, P.J. "The Evolution of Property Rights: A Study of the American West." *Journal of Law and Economics*, 18 (1975): 163-179.

Arthur, John. "Resource Acquisition and Harm." *Canadian Journal of Philosophy*, 17 (1987): 337-348.

Axelrod, Robert. *The Evolution of Cooperation*. New York: Basic Books (1984).

Axelrod, Robert, and Dion, Douglas. "The Further Evolution of Cooperation." *Science* 242 (December, 1988): 1385-1390.

Bagnoli, Mark, and McKee, Michael. "Can the Private Provision of Public Goods Be Efficient? Some Experimental Evidence." *Economic Inquiry*, forthcoming.

Barry, Brian, and Hardin, Russell. *Rational Man and Irrational Society?* Beverly Hills, Calif.: Sage Publications (1982).

Bogart, J.H. "Lockean Provisos and State of Nature Theories." *Ethics*, 95 (1985): 828-836.

Bouckaert, Boudewijn. "Public Goods and the Rise of the Nation State." Unpublished.

Brixey, John C., and Andree, Richard V. *Fundamentals of College Mathematics*. New York: Henry Holt and Co. (1954).

Brubaker, Earl R. "Free Ride, Free Revelation, or Golden Rule?" *Journal of Law and Economics* (1975): 147-161.

Buchanan, Allen. *Ethics, Efficiency, and the Market*. Totowa, N. J.: Rowman & Allanheld (1985).

Buchanan, James M., and Tullock, Gordon. *The Calculus of Consent*. Ann Arbor: University of Michigan Press (1962).

Calabresi, Guido, and Melamed, A. Douglas. "Property Rules, Liability Rules, and Inalienability: One View of the Cathedral." *Harvard Law Review*, 85 (1972): 1089-1128.

Chesher, R. "Practical Problems in Coral Reef Utilization and Management: A Tongan Case Study." *Proceedings of the Fifth International Coral Reef Congress*, 4 (1985): 213-224.

Child, James W. *Nuclear War: The Moral Dimension*, New Brunswick, N.J.: Transaction Books (1986).

Coleman, Jules L. "Market Contractarianism and the Unanimity Rule." *Social Philosophy and Policy* (1985): 69-114.

Coleman, Jules L., and Kraus, Jody. "Rethinking the Theory of Legal Rights." In Jules Coleman, *Markets, Morals, and the Law*. New York: Cambridge University Press (1988): 28-63.

Corbin, Arthur Linton. *Corbin on Contracts*. Vol. 2, St. Paul, Minn.: West Publishing Co. (1950).

Cowen, Tyler, ed. *The Theory of Market Failure*. Fairfax, Va.: George Mason University Press (1988).

Dawes, Robyn M., Orbell, John M., Simmons, Randy T., and Van de Kragt, Alphons J. "Organizing Groups for Collective Action." *American Political Science Review*, 80 (1986): 1171-1185.

De Jasay, Anthony. *Social Contract, Free Ride: A Study of the Public Goods Problem*. New York: Oxford University Press (1989).

Demsetz, Harold. "Toward a Theory of Property Rights." *American Economic Review*, 57 (1967): 347-359.

———. "Why Regulate Utilities?" *Journal of Law and Economics*, 11 (1968): 55-65.

Dorsey, Robert E. "The Voluntary Contributions Mechanism with Real Time Revisions." Unpublished.

Elster, Jon. *The Cement of Society: A Study of Social Order*. New York: Cambridge University Press (1989).

Frank, Robert H. *Passions Within Reason: The Strategic Role of the Emotions*. New York: W.W. Norton Publishing Co. (1988).

Friedman, David. "Comment: Problems in the Provision of Public Goods." *Harvard Journal of Law and Public Policy*, 10 (1987): 505-520.

Friedman, Milton. "The Methodology of Positive Economics." In Milton Friedman, *Essays in Positive Economics*. Chicago: University of Chicago Press (1953): 4-44.

Gauthier, David. *Morals by Agreement*. New York: Oxford University Press (1986).

Goldin, Kenneth D. "Equal Access vs. Selective Access: A Critique of Public Goods Theory." *Public Choice* (1977): 53-71.

Gomez, E.D., Alcala, A.C., and San Diego, A.C. "Status of Philippine Coral Reefs—1981." *Proceedings of the Fourth International Coral Reef Symposium*, 1 (1981): 275-285.

Guttman, Joel M. "A Non-Cournot Model of Voluntary Collective Action." *Economica*, 54 (1987): 1-19.

Hampton, Jean. "Free Rider Problems in the Production of Collective Goods." *Economics and Philosophy*, 3 (1987): 245-273.

Hardin, Garrett. "The Tragedy of the Commons." *Science*, 162 (1968): 1243-1248.

Hardin, Russell. *Collective Action.* Baltimore, Md.: Johns Hopkins University Press (1982).

———. *Morality Within the Limits of Reason.* Chicago: University of Chicago Press (1988).

Hare, R.M. "Ethical Theory and Utilitarianism." In *Utilitarianism and Beyond*, edited by Amartya Sen and Bernard Williams. Cambridge: Cambridge University Press (1982): 23-38.

Harsanyi, John C. "Does Reason Tell Us What Moral Code to Follow and, Indeed, to Follow Any Moral Code at All?" *Ethics*, 96 (1985): 42-55.

Head, John. "Public Goods and Public Policy." *Public Finance* (1962): 197-221.

Hobbes, Thomas. *Leviathan*, edited by Michael Oakeshott. New York: Macmillan Publishing Co. (1962).

Hume, David. "Of the Original Contract." In *Hume's Ethical Writings*, edited by Alasdair MacIntyre. New York: Collier Press (1965): 255-273.

———. *A Treatise of Human Nature*, edited by L. Selby-Bigge. Oxford: Clarendon Press (1978).

Isaac, R. Mark, Schmidtz, David, and Walker, James M. "The Assurance Problem in a Laboratory Market." *Public Choice*, 62 (1989): 217-236.

Isaac, R. Mark, and Walker, James M. "Group Size Effects in Public Goods Provision: The Voluntary Contributions Mechanism." *Quarterly Journal of Economics*, 103 (1988): 179-199.

Isaac, R. Mark, Walker, James M., and Thomas, Susan. "Divergent Evidence on Free Riding: An Experimental Examination of Some Possible Explanations." *Public Choice* (1984): 113-149.

Karelis, Charles. "Distributive Justice and the Public Good." *Economics and Philosophy*, 2 (1986): 101-125.

Kavka, Gregory S. *Hobbesian Moral and Political Theory*. Princeton: Princeton University Press (1986).

———. *Moral Paradoxes of Nuclear Deterrence*. Cambridge: Cambridge University Press (1987).

Klein, Daniel. "Tie-Ins and the Market Provision of Collective Goods." *Harvard Journal of Law and Public Policy*, 10 (1987): 451-474.

Koenig, Richard. "More Firms Turn to Private Courts to Avoid Long, Costly Legal Battles." *Wall Street Journal*. Jan. 4, 1984, p. 27, col. 4.

Kreps, David M., Milgrom, Paul, Roberts, John, and Wilson, Robert. "Rational Cooperation in a Finitely Repeated Prisoner's Dilemma." *Journal of Economic Theory*, 27 (1982): 245-252.

Levin, Michael. "A Hobbesian Minimal State." *Philosophy and Public Affairs*, 11 (1982): 338-353.

———. "To the Lighthouse." *Philosophia*, 19 (1989): 471-474.

Locke, John. *Two Treatises of Government*, edited by Peter Laslett. New York: Cambridge University Press (1963 edition).

Lomasky, Loren E. *Persons, Rights, and the Moral Community*. New York: Oxford University Press (1987).

Luce, R. Duncan, and Raiffa, Howard. *Games and Decisions*. New York: Wiley Publishing Co. (1957).

Mack, Eric. "The Ethics of Taxation: Rights versus Public Goods." In *Taxation and the Deficit Economy*, edited by Dwight Lee. San Francisco, Calif.: Pacific Research Institute (1986): 487-514.

Margolis, Howard. *Selfishness, Altruism, and Rationality: A Theory of Social Choice*. New York: Cambridge University Press (1982).

Mautner, Thomas. "Locke on Original Appropriation." *American Philosophical Quarterly*, 19 (1982): 259-270.

Mill, John Stuart. *On Liberty*, edited by George Sher. Indianapolis, Ind.: Hackett Publishing (1978).

Morris, Christopher W. "A Hobbesian Welfare State?" *Dialogue*, 27 (1988): 653-673.

Miller, Geoffrey P. "Economic Efficiency and the Lockean Proviso." *Harvard Journal of Law and Public Policy*, 10 (1987): 401-410.

Mueller, Dennis. *Public Choice*. New York: Cambridge University Press (1979).

Nagel, Thomas. "Libertarianism Without Foundations." *Yale Law Journal* (1975): 136-149.

Nelson, Alan. "Explanation and Justification in Political Philosophy." *Ethics*, 97 (1986): 154-176.

Nozick, Robert. *Anarchy, State, and Utopia*. New York: Basic Books (1974).

Olson, Mancur. *The Logic of Collective Action*. Cambridge, Mass.: Harvard University Press (1965).

Palmer, Tom G. "Intellectual Property: A Non-Posnerian Law and Economics Approach." *Hamline Law Review*, 12 (1989): 261-304.

Pennock, J. Roland. "Correspondence." *Philosophy and Public Affairs*, 13 (1984): 255-262.

Pettit, Philip, and Sugden, Robert. "The Backward Induction Paradox." *Journal of Philosophy*, 86 (1989): 169-182.

Plato. *Republic*, translated by H.P.D. Lee. Baltimore, Md.: Penguin Books (1955).

Plott, Charles R. "Industrial Organization Theory and Experimental Economics." *Journal of Economic Literature*, 20 (1982): 1485-1527.

Postema, Gerald. "Nozick on Liberty, Compensation, and the Individual's Right to Punish." *Social Theory and Practice* (1980): 311-337.

Rawls, John. *A Theory of Justice*. Cambridge, Mass.: Belknap Press (1971).

Resnick, Michael D. *Choices: An Introduction to Game Theory*. Minneapolis: University of Minnesota Press (1987).

Roberts, Leslie. "Is There Life after Climate Change?" (report from the Conference on Consequences of the Greenhouse Effect for Biological Diversity, Washington, D.C., 1988). *Science*, 242 (1988): 1010-1012.

Roemer, John E. *Free to Lose: An Introduction to Marxist Economic Philosophy*. Cambridge, Mass.: Harvard University Press (1988).

———"A Public Ownership Resolution of the Tragedy of the Commons." *Social Philosophy and Policy*, 6 (1989): 74-92.

Rose, Carol M. "'Enough and as Good' of What?" *Northwestern University Law Review*, 81 (1987): 417-442.

Rosenberg, Alexander. "The Explanatory Role of Existence Proofs." *Ethics*, 97 (1986): 177-186.

Roth, Alvin E. "Laboratory Experimentation in Economics." *Economics and Philosophy*, 2 (1986): 245-273.

Rousseau, J.J. *The Social Contract and Discourse on the Origin and Foundation of Inequality among Mankind*. New York: Washington Square Press (1967 edition).

Sanders, John T. "Justice and the Initial Acquisition of Private Property." *Harvard Journal of Law and Public Policy*, 10 (1987): 367-400.

Sartorius, Rolf. "The Limits of Libertarianism." *Liberty and the Rule of*

Law, edited by Robert L. Cunningham. College Station: Texas A&M Press (1980): 87-131.

———. "Persons and Property." In *Utility and Rights*, edited by R.G. Frey. Minneapolis: University of Minnesota Press (1984): 196-214.

Scheffler, Samuel. *The Rejection of Consequentialism*. Oxford: Oxford University Press (1982).

Schmidtz, David. "Contracts and Public Goods." *Harvard Journal of Law and Public Policy*, 10 (1987a): 475-503.

———. "Deterrence and Criminal Attempts." *Canadian Journal of Philosophy*, 17 (1987b): 615-624.

———. "Public Goods and Political Authority." *Philosophical Papers*, 17 (1988): 185-191.

———. "Contractarianism Without Foundations." *Philosophia*, 19 (1989): 461-470.

———. "Justifying the State." *Ethics*, 101, #1 (1990).

Selten, Reinhard. "The Chain Store Paradox." *Theory and Decision*, 9 (1978): 127-159.

Sen, Amartya. "Isolation, Assurance, and the Social Rate of Discount." *Quarterly Journal of Economics*, 81 (1967): 112-124.

Shand, Alexander H. *The Capitalist Alternative: An Introduction to Neo-Austrian Economics*. New York: New York University Press (1984).

Simmons, A. John. *Moral Principles and Political Obligations*. Princeton: Princeton University Press (1979).

Sitomer, Curtis J. "It's Speedy, Cut-rate, and Confidential: Justice in Private Courts." *Christian Science Monitor*. July 12, 1988, p. 1, col. 2.

Smith, Vernon L. "The Principle of Unanimity and Voluntary Consent in Social Choice." *Journal of Political Economy*, 85 (1977) 1125-1139.

———. "Experiments with a Decentralized Mechanism for Public Goods Provision." *American Economic Review*, 70 (1980): 584-599.

———. "Experimental Methods in Economics." Unpublished.

Sugden, Robert. "Reciprocity: The Supply of Public Goods Through Voluntary Contributions." *Economic Journal*, 94 (1984): 772-787.

———. *The Economics of Rights, Cooperation, and Welfare*. Oxford: Basil Blackwell (1986).

Taylor, Michael. *The Possibility of Cooperation*. New York: Cambridge University Press (1987).

Thomson, Judith Jarvis. "Property Acquisition." *Journal of Philosophy*, 73 (1976): 664-666.

———. *Rights, Restitution, and Risk: Essays in Moral Theory*. Cambridge, Mass.: Harvard University Press (1986).

Trakman, Leon. *The Law Merchant and the Evolution of Commercial Law*. Littleton, Colo.: Fred B. Rothman Press (1983).

Waldron, Jeremy. "Enough and as Good Left for Others." *Philosophical*

Index